DATE DUE			

YOU CAN FLY!

YOU CAN FLY!

Janice Barfield

ZONDERVAN
PUBLISHING HOUSE   OF THE ZONDERVAN CORPORATION
GRAND RAPIDS, MICHIGAN 49506

248. 4
B23 y
130958
Feb 1985

YOU CAN FLY!
Copyright © 1981 by Janice Barfield

Library of Congress Cataloging in Publication Data
Barfield, Janice, 1940-
    You can fly!
        1. Christian life–1960- 2. Air lines–Flight attendants–Religious life.
3. Barfield, Janice, 1940- I. Title.
BV4501.2.B3828   248.4   80-28874
ISBN 0-310-43920-5

Designed and edited by Judith E. Markham

Unless otherwise indicated, Scripture is from the New International Version, copyright © 1978 by New York International Bible Society.

Printed in the United States of America

To the glory
of the Lord Jesus Christ
and to my mother
Lucille Mathis Barfield
who gave me roots
and wings

Contents

Foreword

In the past few years I have had many opportunities to fly as I travel around the country. Yet no matter how many times I hear the roar of the jet engines and the rumbling of the plane speeding down the runway, I am always amazed and intrigued with the world of the airlines.

And the moment my traveling companions and I settle into our seats, the flight attendants are invariably a topic of our conversation. "Look at that stylish lapel pin on her uniform. . . . That uniform is cute, too, isn't it? . . . Boy, she's got a sharp haircut . . . wonder who does it for her? . . . How does she stay so neat and unflappable? . . ." These questions and comments seem rather superficial, but inside I have often wondered about the public and private lives of the women who fly. Is the job really as glamorous as it looks? What about the extraordinary pressures they face as they deal with all kinds of people and situations? How does their demanding schedule affect their relationships with family and friends? Do they ever feel like screaming after they have given that oxygen mask demo for the one-thousandth time and warned us to fasten our seat belts for the ten-thousandth?

Their tailored uniforms and polished professionalism leave us few clues as to who they really are. That's why

I'm so glad my good friend Janice has written this book. She makes it clear that flight attendants are not the exception to any rule—they are ordinary people and they experience the same joys and problems we do. And some are children of God.

Janice shares her walk with the Lord as it is integrated into her life as a flight attendant. Her sensitivity and honesty shine through these pages, and through her experiences we learn much about how to handle our own frustrations, disappointments, joys, and expectations.

Joni Eareckson

Introduction

The story is told of a man who put a cocoon into a glass jar so he could observe its metamorphosis. As he watched the inhabitant of the cocoon squirm and writhe in its imprisonment, he wondered how the exit was ever going to be accomplished. One day the man took his scissors and snipped the confining threads to make the exit just a little easier, and immediately, and with perfect ease, a butterfly crawled out. It had a huge swollen body and tiny shriveled wings, and the man waited anxiously to see the marvelous process of expansion.

He traced the exquisite spots and markings of color which were all there in miniature; he longed to see the creature appear in all its glory. But he looked in vain, for his false tenderness had proved its ruin. The butterfly would never be anything but a stunted abortion, crawling painfully through its brief life when it should have been flying. He had cut short the very struggle that would have prepared the monarch butterfly for flight!

As with the butterfly, there are three phases in the Christian's life. The cocoon stage is the very important beginning. When we come to Christ, we are like babies wrapped in the cocoon of His love. The Bible even says it that way: you must be born again. But the birth is only the beginning. In the safety of that cocoon, we are fed on the milk of His Word. Like babies kept safe from the realities of the grown-up world, we are coddled by God. And we need that very much.

But as we begin to grow, we get restless in that cocoon. And though we never outgrow our need for God's love and nurturing, we long to know more of Him and His ways. One of two things can happen then: we can deny that longing and remain babies in our safe little cocoon, or we can do as Paul says and "grow up in Christ." And that involves struggle. Sometimes it hurts. Badly.

Many times we Christians think that commitment to Christ means a problem-free life. We don't like what is happening to us. We squirm and writhe in our cocoon, feeling overwhelmed by our conflicting emotions. We know that God's Word says, "Consider it pure joy when you face trials of many kinds." But sometimes we don't feel very joyful. And certainly we don't feel safe. Those struggles are painful, and like the man watching the cocoon squirm, we sometimes try and abort our own growth process. We reverse the roles. We endeavor to become our own liberators. The results can be devastating.

But if we hang in there, if we wait for His timing, if we trust God and His Word despite the struggles, despite the failures, despite the fears . . . those very trials can be turned into our good. We can become, by divine process, His monarch butterfly, soaring to heights where only He can take us.

In seventeen years of flying with one of the world's leading airlines, I have lived a life most people only dream about. I've been on a safari in Africa, talked about race horses with the owner of one of the World Series winners, and cracked jokes with Ronald Reagan. I've tried on the ten-carat diamond ring of a millionaire and have had a personal concert by Burl Ives.

But of all the experiences I've had, and am still having, none compares with the fact that I know Jesus Christ. That He is guiding my life with intimate and loving concern.

Many times people have looked at me and said, "You've got it made. You have everything going for you." They don't know about the times I've cried or was tempted to quit. They don't know about the times I've had to stand alone when other Christians weren't around. They don't know about the failures. This book is about some of those times. It's about my struggles in the cocoon.

It's about the flying too. I love Ann Kiemel because she believes the impossible. There are so few people who believe the impossible. Even Christians. Especially Christians. Somehow, in a tiny way, I hope this book will help you believe more in the God of the impossible.

I believe in victory. I really do. But I've learned more from the struggles, because Jesus Christ is right in the middle of them with me! Without the struggles, I would never have been mature enough to fly. And I know the secret: Christ *in* me, my only hope of glory.

You Can Fly*

You can fly but that cocoon has got to go.
You can fly but there are things you've got to know:
The Christian life ain't easy,
It's a far cry from a breeze.
But you can learn to take each headwind down upon your knees.

You can fly but that cocoon has got to go.
You can fly but now your life has got to show
Good signs of a struggle and the bruises that it brings,
For only then you'll find yourself with multi-colored wings.
You can fly!

To fly is your dream,
Freedom is your need.
So keep on keeping on until you succeed.
For the sky is the limit
In anything you do,
So you learn to keep on risking
For that aerial point of view . . . that heavenly point of view.

You can fly but that cocoon has got to go.
You can fly but now you've got to learn to grow.
Fear can keep you grounded, doubt can cloud your sky,
But sipping from the flower of faith can keep you flying high,
Flying high, flying high, flying high.

Words & Music by
Dj Butler

but that cocoon has got to go!

YOU CAN FLY!

My experiences are not worth anything unless they keep me at the Source, Jesus Christ.

Oswald Chambers

I carried you on eagles' wings and brought you to myself.

Exodus 19:4 (NIV)

I've Met
Me a Nut!

*Believe me, every man has his secret sorrows, which
the world knows not; and often times we call a man
cold, when he is only sad.*

Henry Wadsworth Longfellow

My mind was going in a hundred different directions
as I walked through the crowded Atlanta airport that Monday morning. Faces blurred before me as I rushed to meet
my flight. In the fifteen years that I had been a flight attendant I had never gotten used to the continual streams of
people passing each other and yet never knowing or caring
about each other. This particular morning, though, I was
rushing too.

I was excited because during the next month I
would be flying with a good friend. I could hardly wait to
see Jonny. She had become a Christian the year before, and
we were thrilled to be flying together at last.

17

I picked up my pace as the gate came into view. Walking onto the DC-9, I could hear the friendly chatter of Jonny and the other flight attendant, Ann. Shrieks of delight came from my friend and me as we hugged. What could be greater than working all month with a dear friend? And getting paid for it too!

The usual pre-flight procedures began as the three of us decided who would work what cabin. On a DC-9, one person works first class and two work tourist. One of the big jokes among flight attendants is that nobody can ever seem to decide where to start working—especially if the group is congenial and nobody cares. This day was no different. But as much as Jonny and I wanted to work together, we didn't want to seem to exclude Ann. Since Jonny and I were both outgoing, strong personalities, we had decided we didn't want to come on too strong about Christianity. So we agreed to ask the Lord to just love Ann through us. "No sermons, Lord," we promised, "just love in action."

I believe God wants to lead me in every area of my life, and that includes which cabin I am to work. Usually, unless I'm otherwise impressed, I let God speak to me through the other flight attendants as to where I'll work. I take what's left. This isn't being a martyr—it's just fun to see what God will do! That day, I started out in first class.

As I stood at the door, I made a special effort to greet each of the passengers personally while collecting their boarding passes. There were mothers with small children and teen-agers traveling alone, but Monday morning businessmen comprised most of our passenger load.

One of the last passengers to board was a tall, rough-looking man. He was a sharp contrast to the others with his blue denim jeans and jacket. His bleary eyes told me he had probably been drinking. Later, as I took his beverage order, my hunch was confirmed. The others couldn't wait to get their coffee; he wanted a drink.

Our flight was going from Atlanta to Chattanooga to Dayton to Detroit so I had to rush to serve beverages to my fourteen passengers. Flying time to Chattanooga is twenty minutes!

When we arrived in Chattanooga, those who were deplaning did so quickly. They seemed anxious to start their week. *Wish they were this cheerful on Fridays,* I thought. I glanced back to see if everyone had left. There was one person remaining in my cabin, and he was already clamoring for another drink. *Oh, Lord, this is really going to be fun,* I thought. *And he'll probably be my only passenger the rest of the way!*

As I gave the man his drink, we began to talk. He was in the trucking business, and he was going to Dayton. Although he was friendly and even respectful in his coversation, a shiver went up my spine as we talked. He was definitely a man who had seen the raw side of life. I made an excuse to leave as soon as I could.

Sitting on the jump seat for takeoff, my mind wandered back to my drive to work that morning. The fifteen minutes that it takes to drive from my apartment to the Atlanta airport is a perfect time for prayer, and this morning I had had a special prayer request.

My roommate of seven years had moved to Minneapolis two months previously. Her birthday was in a few days, and I wanted to fly up and surprise her. I had waited too late to get a pass. *Guess I'll have to be like everybody else and buy a ticket!* I thought. Because I work for an airline, I could get the ticket at half price, but even then it would be ninety-five dollars. *I don't want to, but I could take it out of my savings,* I mused.

Most of the time my morning prayer begins like this: "Lord, this is (and I say the date). This day has never been except in Your mind. Jesus, live Your life in me today. Take me to the people You would have me minister to today. God, I can't help everybody, but You know who needs a special word or act of kindness. And Father, I need encouragement too. Lead me as You will." More times than I can count God has honored that prayer, and my life is abundant because of His faithfulness.

This Monday morning I had begun in my usual way; then I added, "Father, You know that I want to fly up and surprise Cathy on her birthday, but it costs ninety-five dollars (as if He didn't know!). If you see fit, I would appreciate Your providing that money for me."

Suddenly I was brought back to the present as my one and only passenger leaned out in the aisle and yelled at me, "Do you ever get scared on these things?"

Startled, I said, "I beg your pardon?"

"Do you ever get scared on these things?"

I half smiled as I answered, "Sometimes I do. But I just give it to the Lord, and He takes care of it."

Now it was his turn to be surprised. "What?" he shouted.

"Yes, I do get scared sometimes. But I give it to the Lord, and He takes care of it."

"Well, come over here and tell me about it," he said, patting the seat beside him.

Oh, dear God, I've done it now, I thought. *I don't want to talk to him. God, he's not the kind of person I like talking with. He's coarse and rough. Besides, he's been drinking, and he probably won't even know what I'm saying anyway.* The temptation to sit on my jump seat all the way to Dayton was strong. In fact, I even wished the captain would keep the

20

seat belt sign on all the way so I wouldn't have to get up!

But about that time I remembered the prayer I had uttered that very morning. I had meant it then. Did I mean it now? Sitting there, wrestling with myself, I said, *Father, I don't know what to say to that man. I don't even want to say anything to him. But despite how I feel, I want to be obedient to You. Help me, Lord.* Immediately the seat belt sign went off.

I walked over and sat down beside the half-intoxicated traveler who managed to focus his eyes on my face. "Now, tell me about this religion bit," he said. I began to tell him, as simply as I knew how, that I was committed to Jesus Christ. Then I added, "There's a flight attendant in the back cabin who feels just like I do."

Suddenly he blurted, "Have you ever been to bed with a man?"

Trying not to lose my composure, I looked him straight in the eye and replied, "No, I haven't."

"What!" he shouted. I knew he didn't believe me.

"Well," I began, "my body belongs to God, and I believe that sex belongs to marriage. Since I'm not married—"

"Are you kidding me?" he interrupted. "You've *never* slept with a man?"

Once more I answered, "No."

"How old are you?" the man asked.

"Thirty-seven."

"Thirty-seven years old and a stewardess and you've never been to bed with a man?" he asked incredulously.

"That's right," I replied.

Then my roughnecked, soused, giant of a passenger threw back his head and laughed. "Oh, I've met me a nut!" he said. "I can't believe it, but I've met me a nut!"

Quietly, I tried to talk about my relationship with

Christ, but he asked the question again. *This is getting pretty repetitious,* I thought. So I decided to be just as frank. I knew he must have deep problems.

"Are you married?" I asked.

"Does it look like I've got a wedding ring on that finger? No, I'm not married," he answered softly. I knew I had touched a tender spot so I hurried on while I had the advantage.

"You see, God is the one who invented sex," I said. "It's like a fire He placed inside all of us. If we don't stir up that fire until it's ready to be stirred, then it won't get out of control. What's happening today is that the fire is out of control in lots of people's lives. Sex is using them instead of them using sex."

He looked at me pensively, his eyes clearing. "Yeah, I see," he said quietly. Abruptly he said again, "Oh, but I've met me a nut!" Then he added, "I mean it with respect."

"I know," I said softly.

Actually, I was overwhelmed with the frankness and even the absurdity of our conversation. I wanted to witness for the Lord, but somehow I didn't think it was getting through. And it was becoming embarrassing. I excused myself to do other duties, and as I got up to leave, he said, "Pray for me." There was a hint of sadness in his voice.

"Oh, I will," I promised.

After talking with my first-class passenger, I needed to be reminded of God's love for me. I was not ashamed of what I had told him, but I needed to share it with Jonny, who would understand. As I walked back to the tourist cabin, Jonny and I met in the aisle. I whispered to her, "You won't believe that man up there. Pray for him." And she whispered back to me, "You won't believe what I have to tell you!"

We walked to the back of the plane so we could chat a few minutes. There Jonny told me that when Ann had strolled up to first class my passenger had stopped her and said, "Are you that other religious nut back there?" She came back and told Jonny. His remark then spurred Ann to talk to Jonny about spiritual things!

As we approached Dayton, I returned to my section and sat across the aisle from my passenger.

"I really enjoyed talking with you," I said.

"I enjoyed talking with you, too," he replied. He was quiet now, almost subdued. I wondered what he was thinking. Then my eye caught sight of a folded bill on the empty seat beside him.

I picked it up and handed it to him. "Don't forget your money."

"I want you to have this," he said.

"Oh, no, thank you. You're very kind, but, no, thank you."

His voice was strong. There was no sign of the liquor as he spoke. In fact there was a firmness that surprised me. "I want you to have this," he repeated.

"Thank you so much, but no." I got up then and went to my jump seat for landing.

As I prepared to deplane the passengers, I was afraid he would want to continue the conversation. Instead, he was quite docile. I had even forgotten how big and rough and worn-out he looked. There was a softness about him as he stood towering over me and held out his hand again. "I want you to have this," he said. Once more, I declined.

The airplane door opened about that time, and I turned to greet the agent. I felt a hand put something in my pocket, and my passenger walked off the airplane without another word.

Later, I went into the lavatory to be alone for a few minutes. I didn't have to look in my jacket pocket to know what was there. My mind raced back over the events of the morning. My drive to the airport . . . my prayer for God's provision . . . deciding what cabin I would work . . . not wanting to talk to that man, but doing it out of obedience to God. I thought of my embarrassment at his reaction to me . . . then his changed attitude. And now this.

The Spirit of God overwhelmed me in that tiny airplane lav. All I could do was clutch that hundred dollar bill and cry and praise Him. I was a nut all right—and proud and thankful to be one!*

---

*Delta Airlines' current policy is that money cannot be accepted by flight attendants from passengers for any reason. However, at the time of this incident this was not published as a formal policy.

The Beginning

What is a Christian? The question can be answered in many ways, but the richest answer I know is one who has God for his Father.

J. I. Packer

My twin brother, James, and I were born in 1940 in Marianna, Florida. Seven years later my brother John was born. When I was nine, we moved to Dothan, Alabama.

My mother was a Christian. My father was not. Although daddy didn't claim to believe in Christianity, his attitudes were gentle and loving, and he graciously allowed my mother to bring my brothers and me up "in the faith." It seemed perfectly natural for mother to take us to church while daddy stayed home, but I do remember thinking wistfully at times that I wished he would go with us.

As a young girl, I wanted the most out of life. I wanted freedom, excitement, and love. As far as I was concerned, being a Christian was not the way to get all those things! All about me were the "negatives" of Christianity. Looking back now, I can see that the positives were there too, but I couldn't, or chose not to, see them. At the time what got through to me was DO NOT cheat, DO NOT lie, DO NOT steal, and, above all, DO NOT miss church!

But though I inwardly rebelled against what I thought was the Christian life, I certainly didn't do so outwardly. In fact, my two brothers and I were seemingly so morally good that other people would often point us out as examples. I loved it! But inside something quite different was going on. Terrible thoughts that were not so morally good. And I became fearful that Jesus Christ was going to come back any minute and expose me for what I really was. I was terrified when people talked about "the last days" and Jesus' return to earth.

Although I didn't want to become a Christian (or what I thought was a Christian), I was more afraid *not* to make that commitment. I knew, even in my childish heart, that Jesus Christ was who He said He was. I also knew who I was. And I wasn't prepared to face Him. I was caught between wanting with all my heart what I thought was "the good life" and yielding to Christ for the peace of mind I knew only He could give.

At thirteen, my anguish over my divided self became so great that I did not think I could bear it. That period of my young life caused some of the greatest unrest I ever experienced.

During this time of great dilemma, James and I were sent to a church camp at Perdido Beach, Alabama. And it was at that camp that I finally yielded to Jesus Christ. The surprise of my life came the night I made that total commitment: I found out God loved me!

How many times had I heard that? How many times had I read that in the Bible? How many times had I sung about that love? Hundreds! Yet, for the first time in my life I really knew that *God is Love.* I claimed the truth of P. T. Forsyth's words: "Learn to commit your soul and the building of it to One who can keep and build it as you never can."

Now, instead of dreading Jesus' return, I found myself praying that He would—and soon. I was overwhelmed by His love for me. In fact, I was so thrilled with my new life in Christ that I did a very uncharacteristic thing. I wrote in my Bible, "Saved, July 15, 1954." "Saved" was a Baptist word, or so I thought, and I was not Baptist. It wasn't until later that I learned it is also a very scriptural word!

One of my favorite verses in the Bible is Psalm 31:15: "My times are in your hands." I didn't learn that verse until much later, but the truth of those six words began to make an impact on my young life almost immediately after my conversion. As God's Holy Spirit began teaching me, I saw what a wonderful Father I had. His sense of humor was matchless too! Who else would have put up with my pompous, misguided zeal and loved me in spite of it?

About a year later, a devastating thing happened. Without going into great detail, I will say that my family was shaken to its very roots.

My father had a drinking problem, and he had gotten to the point where he simply could not hold a job to support us. He finally decided he would leave to try and get professional help. My mother let him go in love, and he left in love. He wrote to us several times. Then we never heard from him again.

Many times I would cry, "God, why did You let this happen? Why did You let my daddy leave us?" And sometimes I would be so embarrassed. Everybody I knew had a father. Why were we so different?

Eventually, I began to quit asking God "why" and started thanking Him for the situation. I began to see that God was my real Father and that my only real security was knowing Him as my heavenly Father. I clung to Psalm 68:5: He is "a father of the fatherless." Everyone has to find this out one way or the other. I just had the chance to learn it quicker than most!

Years later, I read in J. I. Packer's book, *Knowing God:* "If you want to know how well a person understands Christianity, find out how much he makes of the thought of being God's child, and having God as his Father." My heart leaped within me as I thought, *Oh, Father, You told me that long ago!*

My mother never tried to take the place of our father. She was a mother to us, and in every sense of the word, she was the very best. She never talked negatively about my dad. When she did mention him, it was only to speak of his good qualities. What a pillar of strength she was!

Providing for three children can be hard enough for two parents, but now my mother had to do it alone. Going back to work after being a housewife and mother for fifteen years was no easy chore, coupled with the constant pain she suffered from a chronic back problem. But her love, cheerfulness, and fortitude were infectious.

Our survival became a family affair, and through our struggles together we became a citadel of love and understanding. My brothers and I did all of the housework and a good deal of the cooking. Most of all, I remember the support and acceptance that we felt from each other and the intense delight we had in simply being together.

Because of our poverty (We didn't think we were poor, by the way; mother had a way of making us feel like royalty.), at one time I didn't have a bedroom. In fact, I didn't even have a bed of my own. I slept on the living room couch that "let out" into a bed. But I remember thinking one night, *Oh, God, I don't even have a bed, and yet I'm so happy. Thank You, Jesus, that You bring me joy, not a bed!* Today, with my well-paying job and my king-size bed, those days seem far away. But I can never thank God enough for teaching me that lesson in the midst of our poverty.

Somehow the bills were always paid, we had a roof over our heads, and plenty to eat (I still remember and *like* those pinto beans!). And, most importantly, we had God and each other.

During those years we lived in rented houses or apartments. Mother used to tell me how she had always prayed for a "home" for us. I assured her that she had given us a home—a real home.

Mother put the clincher on the whole thing years later when she said, "You know, I always wanted a house of our own for you children. But I told the Lord that if we couldn't handle it, not to give it to us." Many times my mother's words come back to me as I pray for something, and I cry out to God, "But if I can't handle it, don't give it to me."

When I graduated from high school and started thinking about the future, I became very confused about what to do with my life. My twin began college. I floundered. I was learning more about God through my relationships with my family and others, and it became increasingly apparent to me that His love for us was what really mattered in life. I desperately wanted to share that love with others. But how?

It was only natural that I would think of becoming a missionary. After all, wasn't that what a really *dedicated* person (especially a girl) was supposed to do? Thus I entered into a period of confusion as to my "purpose" in life. There was no confusion about my relationship to God, just my usefulness to Him. This struggle lasted for over three years.

Finally, one night, the answer came. "You should be an airline stewardess." It was an answer so completely alien to anything I had ever considered that at first I was stunned. It was the wildest, craziest idea in the world. *An airline stewardess? How could I possibly serve the Lord as an airline stewardess?*

All sorts of thoughts danced in my head. And questions! *What a worldly job! What an exciting job! Oh, this can't be for me. It's too exciting, too good to be true!* And later, *What if I don't like flying? What if I get airsick?* On and on they went . . . the questions . . . the "what ifs" . . . the excuses.

Then the Lord said to me, "Janice, I want you to be an airline stewardess and go all over the world and tell people I love them. Tell them joy has nothing to do with circumstances, or people, or anything. Tell them they can rise above all that. Tell them I am their true Father. Tell them I have a plan for their lives. But, most of all, show them My love. Show them by your hard work, your acceptance of them, your cheerfulness, your complete dependence on Me. Show them who I am, Janice!"

And then I laughed. I laughed because God had told

me a secret, and it was so impossible yet so delightful that only He could make it come true. "A *Christian* airline stewardess? Now, really, Lord!" Sometimes even now I laugh because of the seeming incongruity of it all. And a spurt of joy gurgles up within me when I explain to someone on one of my flights how God "called" me to my career.

I remember thinking, *I'll ask my mom, and if she says okay, then I'll know it's from God.* To my amazement, she said, "Fine."

I was on my way. After I made the first application for my "dream" job, I learned one of the most important lessons of my life. God has three distinct answers to prayer—"Yes," "No," and "Wait."

For the next two years I "waited." I had interviews with every major airline in the United States, two interviews with some. Practically everyone in Dothan, Alabama, would go out to the airport to see me off for my interviews. Then there would be the suspense of waiting to hear if I'd been accepted. In this case, no news was bad news. Seven times I waited in eager anticipation, convinced I had the job. Seven times I heard nothing. The silence of rejection almost overwhelmed me. But, I was cheerful—oh, was I cheerful! I'm a very stubborn and optimistic person. And besides, God had "told" me I was to be a stewardess!

It finally dawned on me that I was eating, sleeping, and breathing airline stewardess. I was obsessed with finding God's will for my life. I wanted to tell people about God, so why wasn't He answering? Were my motives pure? *Yes!* Would I give up? *No!* But was I confused? A thousand times *yes!*

After about two years of pursuing my goal, God did a wonderful thing for me. Years later I was to identify what happened to me in the words of Oswald Chambers: "The child of God is not conscious of the will of God because he is the will of God." Up to that point, I had been very conscious of "doing" the will of God rather than "being" the will of God.

I was hanging out clothes for my mom one day when I realized what a fantastic thing it was to know God. I was twenty-two years old, and I knew the Creator of the universe! In fact, He and I were close friends. I remarked out loud, "Why, Lord, knowing You intimately has nothing to do with another person or a place and certainly not a job!" And so, just like that, I gave up. Janice Barfield, with all of her cheerfulness, her fortitude, her good disposition, her love for people, gave up.

And I whispered, "Oh, Jesus, I don't understand. I know You impressed me with this calling; but I want You above everything. I give You any rights I might have taken upon myself, even the right to do Your will. I just want You, Jesus, to live Your life in me."

That was the hardest thing I had ever done in my life. It was even harder than believing on Him as Savior. I knew from the beginning that He was Lord, so I didn't make Jesus the Lord of my life that day. He was already Lord. I just recognized it.

Andrew Murray says, "He knows when we are spiritually ready to receive the blessing to our profit and His glory." My blessing came two weeks after I made that commitment of recognition in the back yard. My younger brother, Johnny, called me at work to tell me the good news, and I made him read and repeat every word over the phone. Delta Airlines had sent me a letter of acceptance! Even now I can't describe the joy I felt. Over and over in my mind the words rolled, *You've been accepted. You've been accepted.*

After I talked with my brother that day, I went off by myself and cried. For twenty minutes I wept with all the pent-up emotion that one can know after two years of constant rejection. I cried because half the town was pulling for me and my dream had become their dream. I cried because I knew I was in the perfect will of God—it wasn't a job that was His will—I was His will.

Most of all, I cried because long ago God had told me He loved me and had a unique plan for my life. Now the plan was unfolding, and I was going to be able to tell the world that God is real! And I was going to fly!

Flight Training

Really, nothing was easier than to step from one rope ladder to the other over the chasm. But, in your dream, you failed, because the thought occurred to you that you might possibly fall.

Dag Hammarskjöld
Markings

Failure must feel very much like drowning. The fear. The grasping. The desperate flailing just to stay above water. And the awful panic when that heavy, ugly monster devours you.

In failure, of course, you survive. At least, usually. Millions do every day. But when you're going down for the third time, other people don't enter your mind. Just the frenzied, animal instinct to stay alive.

Sitting in the classroom near the Atlanta airport with thirteen other young, wide-eyed girls that hot July afternoon, failure was the furthest thing from my mind. I was a winner! As I listened to person after person explain how we had been chosen over so many hundreds of applicants, I became even more convinced of my good fortune. I glanced around the room. Nope! No failures here! And I had made it. Oh, dear God, I had made it.

As we were told what to expect during the next four weeks of intensive training, words such as "equipment," "delay time," and "emergency training" only added to my questions. In time, of course, these phrases would become second nature; but now, how foreign they seemed.

The instructors were gracious and kind and made me feel, if possible, even more excited about being there. We were told that our main reason for being on an airplane was safety for the passengers. Among other things, we would be given training in first aid and emergency procedures. By the time it was over, they promised, they would turn us into real pros. We were to be given eleven tests during the training, and we must maintain a ninety average. Up to that point, I had felt confident. Now a quiver of fear stirred deep inside me.

I remembered another hot afternoon, another classroom . . . five years before. Memories I thought long forgotten stirred deep inside. Past failure raised its ugly head just a smidgen, but it was enough to start me on the road to doubt.

I had wanted to make my mother so proud of me in high school. But I was a "people person"; academics were just not "my thing." Although I was never a particularly good student, I had passed all my subjects. On that spring afternoon, sitting in my high school classroom, my day of reckoning had come.

I had not made good grades in civics—in fact, I had made very poor ones. Then I had failed the final exam. But, I rationalized, so had other people. And besides, we were permitted to take another test.

Now, after taking the make-up test that morning, I waited with a handful of fellow classmates for the results. The fact that I might not graduate never entered my head. Instead, my mind was teeming with graduation plans. Tomorrow I would have my picture taken in my cap and gown. And in three days I would get that long-awaited diploma!

To say I was not prepared for the principal's words is the understatement of the century. When Mr. Jones said, "I'm sorry, Janice, but you didn't pass your make-up exam," I was sure I had misunderstood him. Didn't pass! Impossible! I *had* to pass! My family was coming to see me and my twin brother graduate. I already had my cap and gown. What did he mean, "didn't pass"?

But the looks on the faces of the teacher and the others in the office told me that what I thought impossible was indeed true. For the first time in my seventeen years, my secure little world shattered at my feet, and I fell apart.

I look back now and wonder why that failure affected me so deeply. After all, several years before my family had been torn apart. That had hurt terribly, but it was not like this hurt. Perhaps it was because this hurt was of my own making . . . it was *my* failure.

A deep blackness came over me as I fought to keep my composure, but my grief was uncontrollable. Hot, salty tears gushed from my eyes as I sobbed. It no longer mattered who was in the room with me. All I could think about was my failure. *I* was a failure. I was one big miserable flop in life—at seventeen.

I couldn't begin to think about my mother. She had worked so hard to put me through school. Sacrificed for me. Loved me. Encouraged me. Believed in me. And this was how I had rewarded her. "Oh, God, how could I fail her like this? How could I fail You, Jesus?" The murky waters of defeat overwhelmed me. Hope seemed far away.

Many years later I read in the paper of a seventeen-year-old girl who put a rifle to her heart and killed herself when she learned that she would not graduate with her high school class. The paper said she had tried to tell her parents but couldn't. Ironically, it also said that the parents were "most understanding" after the girl had asked that a counselor call and tell them of her failure. But *she* was the one who couldn't accept the failure. I knew exactly how she felt.

By the providence of God, a teacher friend was in the office that afternoon, and she offered to drive me home. All the way I cried hysterically, saying over and over, "I can't bear to tell my mother." Paramount in my mind was her supposed disappointment in me.

My friend left me at home and went to get my mother at work. As mother walked into the room, it took all my ebbing strength to look into her face and whisper, "I'm so sorry."

She said, "Jan, if this is what it takes to make you wake up and start thinking more seriously about life, then it's worth it." Then she opened her arms to me and said, "I love you."

David Augsburger has said, "It is so much easier to tell a person what to do with his problem than to stand with him in his pain." That afternoon, my mother stood with me in my pain.

There is a wonderful little cartoon titled "Down in a Hole." It shows a stick character looking down at another stick character in a deep cavern. The caption says, "We see a brother or sister in a hole. Our heart goes out to them. We want to help." Then, "So we throw them an answer.

Common answers." The cartoon goes on. "And the answer crushes them." Then it gives some of the answers: "Let's pray" . . . "Try harder" . . . "You dummy" . . . "Have faith." The mood changes as the cartoon continues, "Instead, crawl down into the hole. Embrace the brother or sister—listening, caring." The last picture shows the two stick characters down in the hole together, reaching up toward a ladder. At the top of the ladder, in huge print, is the word HOPE. And the last words say, "And help them find the Christian's hope."

My heart cringes when I recall the times I have been guilty of giving common answers to people in dire need. The times I have been so quick to throw in a specific verse or say, "The *Bible* says." That is not to say that there are not times when this is appropriate. But often I have been insensitive to their pain. I didn't listen to what they were *really* saying. I threw them answers. But, by God's grace, I'm learning.

Later, after I began flying, a tall, lanky, attractive man boarded one of my flights. He looked like a confident businessman. In fact, he had an unusual air of assurance about him. As we approached our destination, the man leaned over from his seat to where I was sitting on the jump seat and started talking about women's lib. The conversation was very casual, yet somehow it came out that I was a Christian.

"Oh," he said, "I know all about that." He went on to tell how he had gone to the altar many times as a teenager to "accept Christ." Then he told me how he and his buddies would do all kinds of wild things. "But I didn't drink, I didn't smoke, and I didn't cuss." It was obvious he knew every Christian "answer" there was. I kept silent as he continued.

"You know," he said, "the only times my father put his arm around me and told me he loved me were when I went forward to be 'saved.'"

I hurt for him when he said that. And I was ashamed for myself and every Christian who at one time or another has done the same thing. I made a new commitment that day to try and really listen to people and to show them love—whether they are "saved" or not.

As our conversation continued, I looked him straight in the eye and said, "I want to ask you one question. Do you have peace?"

He whispered softly, "No, I don't have peace."

I wrote down the titles of three books about people who had experienced circumstances similar to his, men whose lives had been changed by a personal encounter with the living Christ. He took the list and continued to pour out his heart. When he left, he shook my hand and said, "Pray for me."

After my mother, and later my brothers also, so lovingly stood with me in my pain of failure, I turned to the One who understood me even more than they. God was very real to me that evening. And even though I had horrible dreams all night, His presence kept me from going under completely. In one nightmare the principal called my name by mistake when they handed out the diplomas. When the horror of that woke me, my mother was sitting on the edge of the bed holding my hand.

On graduation day I went and sat in the audience. I attended my own graduation, but not as a graduate. It was the hardest thing I had ever done. I knew I would go to summer school and make up my subject; I knew I would get my diploma in six weeks. Despite that, I also knew I had failed my family and myself. But God knew something too!

He knew He could take that failure and make something beautiful out of it. He knew that because of that experience there would come a time when I would be able to sense people were hurting just by looking at their faces. I would be able to spot a "failure" a mile away.

Although I was haunted for years by thoughts of not measuring up, of feeling like a dummy, of insecurity in that area of my life, He knew when and how He would heal me. My struggle to come out of my secure, Christian cocoon had begun.

Now, five years later, as I sat in that stewardess class, my deep feelings of failure began to surface. After all, I had failed once—who was to say I wouldn't fail again? The excited chatter of the girls around me made me wonder if I had done the right thing. After all, they had probably done well in school. What would they think if they knew I had barely gotten by? Most of them had gone to college. After high school, I had gone to work. I had never learned to study in high school and didn't have the benefit of college. How would I ever survive?

The days of classes were long and hard but never boring. I had not realized there was so much to learn about being a stewardess. We covered subjects I had not dreamed were important. Once we got into a discussion about what to do if a woman had a baby. It had happened on several flights, and we had to know what to do! Then there was a whole section on first aid. I never knew there were so many different kinds of fractures and burns. We learned what to do if a person choked on food. All that and much more.

Most of the time was spent memorizing the location and use of emergency equipment on the airplanes. Since Delta had seven types of airplanes at the time, there were myriads of equipment locations to learn. And since the locations varied on each airplane, it was difficult to remember them in a logical manner.

We also learned about the dozens of ways tickets can be issued and the abbreviations of the cities to which our airline flew. As volumes of facts spouted from the instructors, I listened, trying to take it all in. Then I would go home and try to study; but because I had never learned good study habits, it was hard.

After the second test (I made eighty-five on that one and the first one), the instructor called me into her office and kindly but firmly told me I would have to improve. I got desperate! So I did what came naturally. I went back to my room, excused myself from my two roommates, took a pillow into the bathroom, sat on the floor, and prayed. My prayer went something like this: "God, You've brought me this far. And I know You didn't bring me here to fail. Help me, Lord." And then I took my notes and studied harder than I'd ever studied in my life. The next day it paid off. I made a hundred on the test!

I don't remember when I got the idea to cheat. In high school I was so naïve I didn't even know people sometimes cheated. But I did know how easy it was to rationalize. I knew, too, what the Bible says about the heart being deceitful and desperately wicked: ("The heart is deceitful above all things and beyond cure. Who can understand it?" Jer. 17:9.) But I never really believed it about my heart until that day.

I was sitting there, my heart pounding, ready to take the next test. Keep in mind now that I had already seen what God could do when I completely depended on Him in a stressful situation. I knew God hadn't promised me a hundred every time; but He had promised to always be by my side. ("God has said, 'Never will I leave you; never will I forsake you'" Heb. 13:5.) But at that moment I chose to let the fear of failure overrule the peace God had given me just a few days before. It was easy to sneak a glance once in a while at the paper of the girl next to me. . . .

Proverbs 21:2 says, "All a man's ways seem right to him, but the Lord weighs the heart." I was able to take that cheating, which nobody but God knew about, and hide it deep within my heart. But something beautiful inside me began to crack that day. For the first time since I had become a Christian at age thirteen, I deliberately rebelled against God. My Christian principles began to crumble a bit. Oh, I didn't go into years of morbid sin. But I began rationalizing about "little things." I knew what the Bible said about cheating. Repeatedly in Psalms and Proverbs God talks about how He hates cheating and dishonesty of any kind. But, like the Israelites of old, I took things into my own hands. To a degree I was able to push my troubled thoughts away, but my heart began to change.

What shocked me more than my cheating was my rationalizing about it. The only way I could get any peace was to try and push it out of my mind. *Don't think about it. Concentrate on other things.* I was horrified at myself and felt sick inside; yet I was strangely calm. Now my struggle was even greater. Because I had violated my deep beliefs, my sense of failure was compounded. Truly, my heart condemned me.

Somehow, I was able to drive my dark secret even deeper, covering myself with excuses. No one ever knew how disappointed I was in myself. But I knew that God knew, and that knowledge would haunt me, grate on me for eight years before I would do anything about it.

Like Scarlett O'Hara, I would "think about that tomorrow." I had other things to think about now. I was a full-fledged airline stewardess, and I was ready to try my wings!

People . . .
People . . . and
More People!

The world is a looking glass and gives back to every
man the reflection of his own face.
William Makepeace Thackeray

For the first six months of flying, just like everyone else, I was "on reserve." This meant I could be called night or day for a flight. It was fun flying to California or Texas. It was not fun getting up at 4:00 A.M. to do it!

My very first flight took me to Savannah, Georgia, just a few hundred miles from my home base of Atlanta. It was on a Convair 440, and I was the only stewardess on board with forty-four people. I cringed inwardly as I thought of what they might say if they knew it was my first flight. In fact, my greatest fear was that they would find out! The flight went smoothly, however, thanks to my good training and a wonderful crew.

Once in those early days I was serving breakfast from Dallas to Atlanta after flying all night from San Francisco. My task was to serve the beverages. I walked up the aisle with a full pot of coffee in one hand and six glasses of milk on a tray in the other. Just as I was about to pour coffee into a man's cup, the passenger in front of him threw back his head and bumped squarely into my tray! I watched in amazement and unbelief as the startled man was drenched. Apologizing profusely, I ran back to the buffet area and grabbed a handful of towels. I had never spilled anything on anyone, and I didn't know what to expect. Fortunately, the man responded beautifully. In fact, he put me so much at ease that I found myself quipping, "Sir, you've had your milk. Would you like your breakfast now?"

"Yes," he shot back with a grin, "but I'll have my coffee in the cup, if you don't mind!"

The excitement of flying more than made up for the inadequacy I felt scholastically. I knew I was where I belonged. I knew I would do my job well.

And soon I learned that people are very willing to talk on an airplane, probably because they know they'll never see you again. I found myself stretching immensely as a person as I got involved, though briefly, in the lives of my passengers. I couldn't believe people would pour out their lives so readily to someone who was just willing to listen. For the first few years of flying, especially, I felt like the listening ear to half the world. But I was moved greatly by the aching loneliness of many of these people. I felt almost outside myself as they revealed their hearts.

On my first flight to California, I flew out as a stewardess and was supposed to "deadhead" back. When we "deadhead," we fly as a passenger to get back to our home base. When our flight arrived in L.A., I could hardly wait to go into the terminal and check it out for movie stars. After all, I *was* in California! (How naïve can you get?)

While wandering through the airport, I spotted a tall, rugged-looking man dressed in dark clothing. My heart almost stopped. It was Johnny Cash. I stood for a few minutes, trying not to stare. *Well, Janice,* I mused, *you've been to California, and you've seen your celebrity.* Satisfied, I walked back to the gate to board the plane for home.

Since I was deadheading, naturally I was the last person to board. As I strolled up the aisle, I was still excited about my trip to the West, thrilled to have had even a brief visit in California. Then I glanced up and saw an empty seat on the aisle. I couldn't believe my eyes. I blinked to make sure I wasn't dreaming. Sitting in the next seat by the window was Johnny Cash!

Gathering all my courage, yet feeling like the one-month novice I was, I smiled and sat down by the man in black.

"Hi!" he grinned, noting my uniform. "Deadheading?"

His friendly face quickly melted my nervousness, and I spilled out that this was my very first trip to California. He insisted that he change seats with me so I could look out of the window at the scenery on the way.

Then he said, "Oh, my name's Johnny Cash."

"Really!" I exclaimed, feigning ignorance. "I'm Janice Barfield."

For four hours we sat together and talked. He told me how he wrote songs, and I shared some of my dreams about being a stewardess. His sensitivity and graciousness overwhelmed me. That famous man made one little girl feel mighty welcomed into the big world of flying. Several years later I was thrilled to read in the paper that he had committed his life to Christ. But I never did have the nerve to tell him that day that I knew who he was from the beginning!

During those early days I also experienced my first flight in really rough weather. We had served lunch and gathered up the meal trays when the seat belt sign came on. In a matter of minutes, I could tell this wasn't going to be just ordinary "bumpy" weather. Of course, I had only been flying a few months, but I knew it was rougher than usual. I sat down quickly and fastened my seat belt. Glancing around, I saw several people using their little white bags provided in the seat pockets for just such a time.

Memories of my childhood flooded my mind as I remembered how I used to get so carsick. More people were using their bags now as we plowed our way across the turbulent sky. I looked around again, wondering what I should do. I felt fine, but those poor people . . . how could I help them?

I got up and weaved my way to a nice-looking businessman who was using his little bag and looking very sick.

"Excuse me, sir, may I help you?" I asked.

He looked up, trying to keep his composure. "No, I'm fine," he replied. Then he added, "But there's just one thing. My false teeth fell into this bag."

"Oh, don't worry about that." Without thinking further, I said, "Give me the bag," and handed him another one.

I walked to the lavatory with the passenger's ivories in my possession. Suddenly horrified, I thought, *What am I going to do now?* I had no idea how I was going to clean them. *Well, Barfield, you've really done it. Typical maneuver—speaking before thinking. WHEN will you learn?*

Then I remembered that my mother had told me once that when you have children you'll do *anything* for them. I walked into the lavatory and pretended my child had just thrown up.

Without going into details, let me assure you that there *is* a way to get false teeth out of a dirty barf bag without touching them! And there *is* a way to shut your mind out and do your duty! My biggest problem then was that I hadn't been around long enough to know the difference between duty and stupidity! But later, when I gave the man his spotless teeth back in a clean bag, his toothless smile of thanks was enough for me. Just don't ask me if I'd do that now!

There were many special times. There were good spiritual times when I was able to share my relationship with Christ. And there were delightful little surprises that only God could have planned. Once I helped an elderly man onto the airplane and to his seat. He had a slight build and a thick accent. Later, I heard him say that his name was Niebuhr.

"Oh, there's a very famous theologian by that name," I told him.

"I am he," he replied with a smile. What a wonderful conversation we had that day as I plied him with questions and Reinhold Niebuhr told me about the time he had preached in Red Square in Moscow on Easter Sunday.

Another time when my roommate Laurie, who was also a believer, and I were flying together, she spotted a man reading a book by a contemporary writer. We had both read some of the author's works and knew her writing was purely humanistic.

"I've read that book," I told the man when I had occasion to pass his seat.

"It has all the answers I've been searching for," he said.

"Oh, well, it's interesting, but we've found something more." Laurie was standing beside me now. We smiled at him and walked to the rear of the plane to finish our work. In a few minutes, our passenger had joined us. He was full of questions.

"What do you mean, 'something more'? How can you be sure you're so right in your thinking?" For some time we were able to share with the man about the Person of Jesus Christ. He asked deep questions. What I couldn't answer, Laurie could. Though neither of us considered ourselves intellectuals, somehow we were able to answer to the man's satisfaction every question he posed. I've never forgotten his name, and I pray for him to this day.

One day on the long flight from Atlanta to Los Angeles, I walked by a man who was sitting in the back of the Stretched DC-8 and noticed a book of poetry on the seat beside him.

"Oh, you like poetry?" I asked.

"Yes," he replied. "In fact, I wrote this. It's just come out."

The plane wasn't full that morning, so I sat down to talk a few minutes and shared with him that I, too, wrote poetry. He said, "I'd give you this book, but it's the only one I have." I protested that I wouldn't even hear of it but thanked him for his kind thought.

After finishing my meal service, I went back to talk some more. It didn't take more than a few minutes to discover what a fascinating person he was. He was from England and was a professor at Cambridge University. I asked if he had heard of C. S. Lewis and was thrilled to learn that my passenger had studied under the famous don. Needless to say, I asked him all kinds of questions about Lewis.

Soon we were talking like buddies. Although we could not meet on an intellectual level, a bond quickly formed as we shared our mutual interest in writing. He was not a believer but listened with interest as I wrote down some of my Christian poems for him. Then he read to me from his new book. Before the flight was over, he had not only given me his book of poetry, but had autographed it and then written a poem on the back page—just for me!

I learned a lot about communication that day. A listening heart has no intellectual barriers.

As I said earlier, from the very beginning of my career as a stewardess I found myself really getting involved with some of my passengers. Little old ladies are my specialty, and I've had more than one kiss me good-by as she deplaned.

Once an agent helped an older woman on board. She was sobbing softly as he took her to her seat in the first class section of the DC-9. He explained to us that the passenger's grandchild was on board—in a casket in the belly of the plane. My heart ached for her as I walked back to tourist to get ready for the flight.

My mind teemed with thoughts of that dear bereaved woman as I went about my duties. I could not forget her. Finally I felt prompted by the Lord to speak to her. Breathing a quick prayer, I headed up front.

I said the first thing that popped into my head as I sat down beside her. "I just want you to know that I'm praying for you."

She looked at me and said, "Honey, I'm a Christian also." Then for several minutes she poured out her grief. I soon had to return to my passengers, but occasionally I would go up and check on her and offer a word of encouragement. Her countenance changed during the flight as she drew upon God's promise of peace.

When we got to our destination, I walked up to the microphone to make the final announcements.

"Welcome to Shreveport, ladies and gentlemen. Be sure and check in the overhead racks and all around you for any personal *problems* you might have brought on board." Then I froze. Had I actually *said* "problems" or was I just thinking it?

When I went to tell my new friend good-by, she embraced me warmly before she walked off the plane. None of my fellow crew members had said anything about my announcement. Maybe I was safe. About that time one of the deplaning passengers turned around and laughingly said, "What's that about checking for *personal problems?*"

I grinned back at him. I might have messed up on the PA, but my heart was in the right place. In the days to come, as now, God constantly confirmed in a deep way what He had impressed upon me years before when I had sought His "purpose" for my life. Flying would never be "just a job" for me.

Clear
Conscience . . .
Clear Future

We do not lose peace with God over another person's sin; but only over our own. Only when we are willing to be cleansed there will we have his peace.

Roy Hession

Despite the exciting time I was having in my profession and despite the way God was working, there was a vague discontentedness inside me. Occasional uncomfortable thoughts ran through my mind. These thoughts always pertained to my feelings of inadequacy and failure, and at the bottom of them all was my cheating in stewardess school. Sometimes the guilt and shame seemed unbearable, and I cringed at the thoughts. But somehow I always managed to push them down deeper into my heart. I even rationalized that someday I might get married and quit flying. Then I would go to my instructor and confess what I had done. This superficial salve worked for a number of years.

Suddenly time caught up with me. I had been flying for eight years and was ready for a change. My roommate, Laurie, had long since moved to Miami, gotten married, and quit flying. In fact, most of my friends had married and settled down. I would have little conversations with the Lord: "Now, God, I know that You led me into this job. I've been doing this for a long time now. But, really, don't You think it's time I settled down and got married?"

During this period of my life I went to Dallas to visit a friend. My friend was also thinking about changes in her life, and we both speculated as to what God might have in store for us. A couple of hours before she took me to the airport, she casually told me about a seminar she had attended. As I picked up the seminar notebook she had been given and flipped through it, my eyes fell upon a page about clearing your conscience. Gulping hard, I put the notebook down on the sofa. I didn't need that. Not now. My defenses were too well built. But I couldn't resist asking her about some of the things she was learning. God had some changes in store for me all right, but they weren't exactly what I had in mind!

A few weeks later I was sitting in church. I attended a wonderful church where the fellowship was warm and the pastor, Dr. Sandell, preached straight from the Bible. I usually clung to every word he said. That night, however, my mind kept wandering. Suddenly, he started telling a story that got my attention: Dr. Sandell told of a preacher in Canada who had prayed for revival to come to his church. God's Spirit got hold of the preacher and impressed upon him that before he could have revival in his church, he had to have revival in his own life. I sat up straighter then, and although I was afraid of what I would hear, I felt strangely compelled to listen. I *had* to hear the end of that story.

"Then," Dr. Sandell continued, "this minister started repenting of sins in his life. God brought to mind people he had hurt, wrongs he had done."

Oh, God, that's me, I thought. A sharp, uneasy pain began to rise within me.

Dr. Sandell went on to tell how the Canadian minister had gone back to shopkeepers, bank tellers—all kinds of people he had wronged—and asked for their forgiveness.

Later during the service as we were singing the last hymn, hot tears flooded my eyes. The conviction of sin in my life was inescapable. All I could see was the face of Jesus in all of His purity and honor, and I saw how I had hurt Him. I knew I had sinned against my instructor, the girl from whom I had cheated, and myself. But my greatest sin was against God, even Jesus Christ, the perfect God-Man who had become sin for me. From the bottom of my heart I cried out to Him: "Against Thee, Thee only have I sinned, and done this evil in Thy sight."

Standing there in church on that Sunday night, I made a choice. The only thing that mattered to me was to be right with God. To be at peace with Him. To be able to look Him in the face without shame or regret. Whatever it took, I was prepared to do. And I knew in my heart what I had to do.

That night I went home and slept like a baby. I had repented of my cheating to the Lord, and God had assured me of His forgiveness. Now I had to make it right with others.

The next morning I called my former instructor and made an appointment for later that day. Then I clung to the Word of God as I never had before. Down on my knees, I cried out to God: "Lord, I cannot do what I am about to do without Your help. Please, dear Father, speak to me through Your Scriptures." Even though I didn't know what was going to happen to me, my heart was full of praise to the Lord. I could truly say with Jeremiah, "Heal me, O Lord, and I will be healed; save me and I will be saved, for you are the one I praise" (Jer. 17:14).

I was reading one of Oswald Chamber's devotional books at the time. The passage was from Isaiah 40:1-2, and this was his commentary:

> "Comfort ye, comfort ye My people, saith your God." Notice the "My" and remember that they were a disobedient people, and yet God is not ashamed to be called their God. It is not the love of God for a pure saint, but the love of God for a sin-stained people. He might well have been ashamed of them on account of their sin and degradation, but His voice comes in all its amazing wonder—"Speak ye comfortably" (to the heart of, R.V. margin) "to Jerusalem. . . ."

I don't think I have ever been as aware of the love of God as I was that day—a deep sense of love and forgiveness such as I had never known before. I picked up the Living Bible then and read the complete two verses. They thrilled me even more: "Comfort, oh, comfort my people, says your God. Speak tenderly to Jerusalem and tell that her sad days are gone. Her sins are pardoned, and the Lord will give her twice as many blessings as he gave her punishment before."

After praying with a heart overflowing with praise, I was ready for my appointment.

The words I said to my instructor that morning aren't important, but I made my tearful confession. I told her I was going to ask forgiveness of the girl from whom I'd cheated. I had lost touch with her, but I knew God would help me find her. There would be a way.

The instructor's response was beautiful. We talked quietly, intensely, and then she asked, "When did you make this decision about Jesus Christ?" When I told her I had been thirteen and how serious I was about my commitment and the anguish my sin had caused me, she said, "I don't know how you stood it all this time." I will always be grateful to that lovely woman for her sensitivity to me at that moment. Her reaction could have been so different. For the second time in my life, another human being stood with me in my pain. And it made all the difference in my life.

Years later, I found a poem by Renee Ashby that best describes how I felt that day. It's called "Restoration."

> Just now came
> rushing back to me
> a thousand memories
> of beautiful times
> amazing deliverances
> peace beyond words
> exciting joyous times
> totally liberating
> when all i could do
> was cry
> and sing
> praises to Your name.
>
> Restored
> at this point in eternity
> are all those joys
> and anticipations
> of the pure
> just-like-in-Acts
> excitement
> of living a life
> controlled by You
> of walking a path
> prepared by You.

Restored
at this moment in my life
that carefree heart
experience
of knowing that all is
Yours to command
Beloved of the King
of the universe:
like the feeling i had
as a child
when school was out
for the summer.

O Jesus
the summer
of my life.
The Author
Finisher
and Restorer
of my Joy.

As I walked out into the crisp, cool Georgia air that day, I felt as if a huge boulder had been lifted from my shoulders. I walked with the step I had known as a teenager who had just found God. To have a pure heart again . . . a clear conscience. Oh, dear God! It was wonderful! I laughed and cried at the same time. If anyone had seen me, they would have thought I was in love. And I *was* in love! I was in love with the Creator of the universe. I had seen Him and I had seen myself in a unique way. And I knew my life would never be the same again. My spiritual wings were stretching, and my *real flying* was just about to begin!

The Role Conflict

*We are not pulled from behind, but lured from be-
fore! Not pushed, but pulled! Magnetized from beyond!*

Lloyd C. Douglas

I knew the moment I tacked the poster on the big
bulletin board in the stew lounge in Atlanta that I was
tacking my reputation up beside it.

INTERESTED IN CHRISTIAN FELLOWSHIP AND
SHARING? CONTACT JANICE BARFIELD.

A year before, a Delta captain named Joe Ivey had
started a Christian fellowship for the pilots on the airlines;
now twenty-five or so attended a monthly luncheon meeting. Joe was a tactful, loving, yet firmly committed Christian. He and his wife Barbara were my kind of people, and
we had had good fellowship together.

59

Many times I'd tell him, "Joe, I don't know of any women in the airlines who really stand up for Christ." Actually, at the time it never dawned on me that there could be many other girls in my position—waiting for someone else to take a stand. It certainly never occurred to me that God might want *me* to be that someone.

Now that my conscience was clear, I saw my job in a whole new perspective. And a few weeks after confessing to my instructor, God laid on my heart a desire to really count for Him in my job. Two women in my church—Julianna, an Eastern Airlines stewardess, and Patty, an ex-Eastern stew—helped give me the courage to do something definite. One evening the three of us had dinner at my apartment. Afterwards we prayed and asked God to use us for Him in the airlines. "We'll do whatever *You* tell us, Lord." We decided that the best thing would be to just put up a notice on the bulletin board.

So here I was a few days later, putting up this sign. Delta had given me permission; Julianna had Eastern's okay to tack up the same notice in their stew lounge. I was scared to death, not knowing what to expect.

I had never tried to hide the fact that I was a Christian, but this was different. This time it involved my job and my reputation with the other stewardesses. Christianity is often acceptable until you try to involve others; it's at that point that you become "odd." I didn't want to be odd, but I knew this was something I had to do. I breathed a silent prayer as I left the lounge. *Well,* I thought, *it's all or nothing!*

A few days later I began to get telephone calls and notes. Christians were coming out of the woodwork! There were positive responses and cautious ones. I remember one note in particular: "I wouldn't take the prize for the best

Christian, but I *am* interested." But the gist of most responses was: "I've been waiting for something like this!" I could hardly believe the interest and hunger for Christian fellowship among these women. My heart was thrilled. Now that I was able to believe God for the impossible, it was happening.

A month later we had our very first "Fellowship of Christian Stewardesses" meeting. Joe and Barbara Ivey came along with fifteen others—all stewardesses who were interested in the things of God. From the beginning we were direct and honest and firm. The goal Captain Ivey shared that day has remained our goal through the years: to lift up Jesus Christ on the airlines by being a positive example and to be an encouragement to believers.

After the initial meeting, I led the women's group every month at a luncheon meeting in a local cafeteria. We had stewardesses and office people from several airlines. Joe continued to lead the men. Soon other airline personnel were joining us; mechanics, secretaries, and reservation people became a regular part of our groups. After a year of meeting separately in Atlanta, the men and women and their spouses started meeting together.

God began doing exciting things in the airlines, and we saw Him touch many lives. Soon the Iveys were getting mail from all over the country. People were hearing that there was a group of Christian airline personnel in Atlanta and wanted to know more about it. Then we heard that people in other airlines were doing the same thing. People in Chicago and Minneapolis. Letters poured in asking what was going on. The answer was simple: we were just a group of Christians meeting together to share our walk with Jesus Christ. And we happened to work for the airlines.

In January of 1973, Joe Ivey contacted all the airline

people he had heard from during the past couple of years. He sent out a hundred invitations to people all over the country to meet in the Ivey home and talk about ministry within the airlines. Fifty people came from as far north as Minneapolis and as far west as Los Angeles. A Christian lawyer from Chicago flew down to do our legal work. After three days of talking, fellowship, and much prayer, it was decided that we would officially be known as The Fellowship of Christian Airline Personnel. There would be no dues, no membership regulations, and no mandatory attendance. God had called us together; He would provide the funds. We drew up a biblical statement of faith and elected a board of directors and an advisory board. Joe Ivey was elected president.

I stood back in awe as I observed all of this. My mind was reeling at the goodness of God. I had taken one step of obedience in faith and the next thing I knew I was in the middle of a movement of God in an area that had never been touched to such a degree by Him. And I was very aware that it was His doing and not mine. I had seen where my planning could take me. Now my heavenly Father was mapping out His plan for me.

Oswald Chambers says that when we deliberately decide to obey God, He will tax the remotest star and the last grain of sand to assist us with His almighty power. I was experiencing that power as I saw God doing a unique work.

I still chuckle at some of the rumors that circulated in those early days of our meeting together. Someone told one of the stews that she heard our group had taken a vow never to marry. Of course, some of our people were already married and many were engaged or dating someone special, so we never did figure out how that one got started! Then someone said that they heard we sat around on the floor in a circle and said "Hallelujah and praise the Lord" for three hours. We did pray a lot, and many of those prayers were being answered. And a lot of praises went up to the Lord. But, three hours of two phrases? Rumors! It was interesting to note, however, that none of these rumor-makers ever attended our meetings.

Once a flight attendant said to me, "Janice, what do you do when they say all of those things about you?"

"What things?" I laughed. I had no idea what she meant at the time.

"Oh, when they call you a fanatic," she said.

Later, I read a verse from the Psalms that reminded me of our conversation: "In the shelter of your presence you hide them from the intrigues of men; in your dwelling you keep them safe from the strife of tongues" (Ps. 31:20). I know God has protected me from so much. Not that I'm living a sheltered life. But God is keeping my life in His secret *shelter* and I can be sure that whatever I do hear He has allowed me to hear. The psalmist also says: "He who dwells in the shelter of the Most High will rest in the shadow of the Almighty" (Ps. 91:1). I can rest in the fact that God orders my circumstances.

But taking a stand for Christ does involve risk. Writing this book involves risks. In fact, it took me years to get the courage to do it. What if I pour my heart out to you and you don't understand? What if my liberal friends think I'm too conservative and my conservative friends think I'm too liberal? Worse still, what if you think that what I have to say is silly or meaningless? I have struggled with all these questions.

Several years ago I read a Bruce Larson book, *No Longer Strangers*. It helped me tremendously in my struggle to come out of the cocoon. God used the truths in it to show me what the Christian "flight" is all about. Larson spoke of vulnerability and affirmation and shared how Jesus chose to be vulnerable for us on the cross by taking on all of the sins of humanity. Christ became a prostitute, a thief, a liar—for you, for me. He not only paid the penalty for our sins, but also identified completely with us as human beings. When I cheated in stew school, I was shocked at myself. But He wasn't shocked at me. When He was crucified nearly two thousand years ago, He paid for every sin I have ever committed or ever will commit. When I choose to trust in that payment with all my heart, it makes me right with God.

Then Jesus does the ultimate: He affirms me as a human being made perfect by Him when He rose again! When I see who He is, the perfect Godhead made sin for me, I can *dare* to be vulnerable with you. Not because of who I am, but because of who He is!

As I think of that Easter morn when Mary went to look for her Lord at the tomb and found Him missing, my heart runs with her as she scampers to tell the others. The unthinkable had happened. Jesus lived with them, knew them, died for them . . . and came back again. Despite what He knew about them, He came back! He came back for you, for me. I don't know about you, but that fact gives me the confidence to want to shout to the world who He is. That kind of love affirms every fiber of my being.

In his book, Larson went on to explain that we, too, can choose to become vulnerable to each other. We can open ourselves up to others and, in doing so, affirm each other.

When I let one of my close stewardess friends read my chapters on "Flight Training" and "Clear Conscience" she said, "You know, I really can't identify with your deep feelings of failure even though I can appreciate how you feel." When her husband, who was working on his Ph.D. in psychology read it, he asked, "Is *that* the worst thing you've ever done?"

What they were both saying, of course, is that a lot of people seemingly have done much worse things. Almost every day I fly with or meet people who live with unbelievable guilt. Some have had abortions. Some have given away illegitimate children. Some are homosexuals. Some are having affairs and are trying to end them. Some are having affairs and don't want to end them. But God places no degree on sin. Sin is sin. To the Lord of Truth, a "little white lie" is the same as a great big one. And stealing time on the job is just as bad as the Brinks robbery.

But the most surprising reactions to my Christian stand came from other Christians. For the first time in the eight years I had been flying, I was questioned as to my choice of career. The first time this happened, it came from—of all people—another stewardess! During a flight, we had gotten into a conversation about Christianity. She was a Christian but didn't seem to share the same views I did about being committed to Christ on the job.

The next day as we were working, she said casually, "My husband and I were talking about you last night, and he says you can't be a committed Christian and be in this job. He says that's like (and she named a well-known minister) going into a bar, having a scotch and water, and saying, 'Let's talk about Christ.'"

I was startled at her comments and didn't know what to say for a few minutes. Then I spoke, weighing every word. "You know, your husband doesn't know me. He doesn't see deep inside my heart. I appreciate his views, but how can he tell what's right for me? That's for God to say."

YOU CAN FLY! 65

We were working tourist on a DC-9 that day, and it was time for me to take my turn in first class. I was the only stew up there, so I had plenty of time to think. A deep heaviness settled on me. An oppression. All sorts of questions ran through my mind.

Lord, maybe she's right. Maybe I can't be committed to You and be here. Maybe I'm just a stumbling block to people. My mind whirled as I thought of my job in relation to God. Above all, I wanted to be obedient to Him. I became more confused by the minute.

Then I remembered something a dear friend had told me several years before. "Sometimes we don't know if a thought is from God or from Satan. Especially if there is no direct Scripture about it." She said that people can prove anything by taking verses out of context, then followed that statement up with some sound advice.

Now I thought about the advice my godly friend had given. I wanted to know what was right for *me*. So I decided to do what she had suggested. Sitting there on the jump seat, thirty-five thousand feet up, I prayed, "Lord, if this is from You, then I embrace it. If You don't want me here, I'll quit." Then I took a deep breath and said, "But, Satan, if it's from you, in the Name of the Lord Jesus Christ, I refuse it!"

Immediately, the heaviness left and God's peace flowed through me. I knew I was where He wanted me. Other believers might not feel free to be in my job. And tomorrow, or in a few years, He might lead me somewhere else. But for now, the conviction of being in the right place was there. That determination to follow Him no matter what the cost was driven deeper still.

As I sat there thinking about God and His love and leading for me, a strange thing began to happen. Thoughts of my brothers and sisters in the airlines began to come to me. I wondered if they ever encountered what I had just experienced. Love welled up inside me as I prayed for them and any problems they might be having at that time. I felt overwhelmed with concern for them and wanted to encourage them. There was a deep sense of their presence with me.

"Oh God, encourage them. Love them, Lord," I prayed. And I felt supported by them as though they knew what I had just been through.

Keith Miller speaks of this very thing so beautifully in the book he and Bruce Larson wrote, *The Passionate People,* when he talks about how important it is to feel the acceptance of other Christians that you are close to in a small group. He refers to Carlyle Marney's idea that the Freudians had emphasized the point that we are controlled by "basement people" from our past who go with us everywhere and whom we blame for reaching up out of our subconscious to push us off our best trails. "But," Miller continues, "we Christians have another powerful kind of influence available to us: people who love God and love us and who go with us in an imaginary balcony on the inside wall of our minds. And they cheer us on to be loving and like Christ when we are out in the world alone . . . and are tempted to cop out." He also believes that the saints in the Bible and in the church's history can become part of our balcony people. Through their written words they urge us to keep the faith and to love people out in the world.

As a result of that conversation with my skeptical co-worker, I realized how deeply I wanted to be liked and accepted. Especially among Christians. And even more so by my own kind, evangelicals. My attitude had been one of "stand and defend," saying to anyone who would listen,

"Look, I'm just as evangelical as you are. My commitment is deep. My life is Jesus Christ. Please understand me." But I was becoming painfully aware that I could survive even if people of my "own kind" didn't understand.

Another way the Lord used others' criticism of me was to make me aware of my own critical attitude. This first came to my attention when a man from my church was on my flight and I noticed he had a martini sitting in front of him. My mind whirled as I thought, *How can he be a committed Christian and have that drink?* Just then the Holy Spirit gently nudged me and whispered, "Janice, you're judging him." My face flushed as I remembered what God was so painfully teaching me. Who was I to condemn this man? I was horrified and embarrassed at my judgmental and critical thinking, but I knew God was teaching me more about myself and my own attitude toward other Christians.

Several years ago I attended a Christian publications' convention in a large northern city. I was representing our monthly newsletter for the Fellowship of Christian Airline Personnel, *The Trim Tab.* Top writers and editors of Christian magazines were there, and I was thrilled to be able to meet and talk with them.

As I walked out of a session one morning, the editor of a denominational magazine, with whom I had been in a prayer group, came up to me. Without a word of greeting, he said, "What do you girls do when you have to serve liquor?"

He asked an honest question. I gave him an honest answer. "Well, it's part of our job. We serve it."

"There's a church in our denomination that won't give membership to Shakey Pizza Parlour people or airline stewardesses," he replied.

I felt condemned and mumbled something about

how that was between them and the Lord. But I couldn't help thinking of my dear stewardess friends who might be kept out of God's house by such attitudes.

Even though at the time I felt this man was being judgmental of me, I don't blame him now for what he said. He was simply stating a fact about one church. It is a position with which I strongly disagree, but I realize that my job will always be a bit controversial to some people. In some Christian's eyes there will always be a "role conflict."

Some time ago I received a scorching letter from a lady of my own denomination who ripped me apart for saying I was committed to Christ while "you do the job you do." She proceeded to name all the things in my work that "keep you from God." I wrote her back, explaining how God had led me into airline work. I told her she would be thrilled to see what the Lord was doing in the lives of airlines personnel. She quickly replied, raving even more and using everyone from my pastor to the founder of my denomination in evidence against me. "They don't stand for what you are doing . . . how can *you?*" (I never did write back and tell her that there are many flight attendants in my church and that my pastor and his wife are among our most loving encouragers!) She ended her tirade by saying, "I suggest, Miss Barfield, that you examine yourself to see if you are in the faith."

My heart goes out to that woman. She had a right to her opinion, but her problem was not with me, although she thought it was. Her letter was full of bitterness and hate. I think of her and others like her and thank God for getting my attention to pray for them, even if it means being the recipient of unkind letters and remarks.

But I am at peace. I enjoy my job more than ever. I don't drink, but I feel free before the Lord to serve liquor in my job. Some people would not feel comfortable in my job, and I can accept that. I am convinced of the absolute necessity of living by our personal convictions, not by somebody else's. We can look to other Christians for advice, but ultimately we have to answer to God, not to other people. I am also convinced that the only way we can have the courage to stand by our convictions, especially when they differ with those of someone whom we greatly admire and love, is to know that we have God's approval in our life. And the Bible says He will tell us what to do if we ask. ("If any of you lacks wisdom, he should ask God, who gives generously to all without finding fault, and it will be given to him," James 1:5.)

Remember the ex-Eastern stew who met with Julianna and me before we put up those posters? She quit the airlines after she became a Christian because she didn't feel free to serve liquor. But Patty loves me and I love her. We don't condemn each other. We're both trying to be what Jesus wants us to be. God led her out of the airlines. He left me in.

It is enough for me to have my "balcony people" and those dear members of the body of Christ whose attitude is: "A *Christian* stewardess? What an opportunity!" Most of all, there is God's peace. No "role conflict" for me!

I love the section in John where Peter is questioning the Lord about the other disciples. He speaks for us all when he says, "Lord, what about him?" And Jesus so wonderfully answers: "If I want him to remain alive until I return, what is that to you? You must follow me!" (John 21:21-22).

In the days to come, God may want me to remain or go. But whatever surprises He has in store, I'll follow Him!

Myth of the "Sex Symbol" Stewardess

Your capacity to say no determines your capacity to say yes to greater things.

E. Stanley Jones

My very first airplane ride gave me the clue. One of the major airlines had sent me a free pass to fly down to Miami for an interview. I was excited, nervous, and as naïve as they come.

As I boarded the little Convair 440, I glanced back over my shoulder. Half my hometown had come to see me off. I settled into my seat as the stewardess walked by to check seat belts. My mind began to wander as all sorts of questions filled my head. What was I getting into?

I was startled later when the stewardess stopped by my seat to chat. She knew I was going for a job interview and was sensitive to my nervousness. She seemed happy to answer my multitude of questions about flying. About that time the captain came over the P.A. announcing some rough weather in the area. Because of it, we were to stop in Tampa first and then go on to Miami.

Since there was a possibility that the flight might not go on to Miami because of the weather, "Sam" (short for Samantha), my stewardess, took me off the plane with her. Walking into the crew lounge with a real stewardess, I felt like a celebrity. All around me were pilots and other crew members—people I had seen only in the movies or in my dreams. My new-found friend explained to me that if my flight was canceled I could go home with her to her Tampa apartment. Her kindness touched me deeply.

Just then the captain of our flight walked over and interrupted our conversation. Tall, good-looking, and the prototype of a "swinger," he put his arm around me and said loud enough for everyone to hear, "Oh, come on, Sam, what's her mother going to think when she calls home and says she's spending the night with Sam?" I flushed, not knowing what to say.

He continued, "She might as well spend the night with me. She'll have a lot more fun."

Hence, my introduction to the world of the sex-symbol stewardess.

After I started flying, I was constantly bombarded with sexual remarks. It didn't take long to learn, however, that if I acted like a lady, I would be treated as one. Usually!

But it was rough being a "greenhorn" and not knowing what to say to the guys who made such overt comments. Yet I saw the Lord work even in those situations. One trip is especially clear in my memory.

I was the only stewardess on the Convair 440, and it

was my third day of flying with this particular captain. He was pleasant, but he knew I was young and new, and he played it to the hilt. As I look back now, I realize that today it would be considered sexual harassment on the job. But I didn't know how to handle it then. I tried to get along with him, but it was difficult for me to take his constant needling about sex.

Finally tears came to my eyes as I sensed my helplessness. "Lord," I prayed, "please do something . . . anything . . . just get me through this flight."

About that time we arrived at the next stop on our "puddle hop," and I deplaned the passengers. As the new passengers came aboard, I spotted a familiar face. I could not recall his name or even where I had met him until I walked by his seat later and saw him reading the Bible. Then I remembered that I had heard him speak about a year before; I remembered his enthusiasm and strength as he talked about Jesus Christ. I introduced myself to him, and as we chatted I was awed by the fact that God would send me this word of encouragement so quickly. The past few days were now put in proper perspective.

Elated, I ambled back to the galley, thanking God over and over for the miracle of answered prayer. Suddenly a thought ran through my head: *If you think that's an answer to prayer—that God sent this man to encourage you—share it with your new friend.*

As I related my story to the man, he threw back his head and laughed. Seeing my puzzled expression, he quickly explained. "You know, when I got on this plane I was mad." While sitting in the coffee shop of the airport, he had heard them call another flight that was a nonstop flight to his destination. This flight that he had been booked on stopped twice before it got to his home. The other flight

YOU CAN FLY! 73

would have been ideal for him because he had two speaking engagements yet that afternoon. "Lord," he had prayed, "I don't know why You want me on *this* flight, but I'm going."

Now it was my turn to laugh. It was clear to both of us why he was there. For the first time in my flying career I saw God answer a specific prayer for help in my job.

Let me hasten to explain that not all crews are like that one. And although crew members can be a problem sometimes, so can the passengers. And some flight attendants can be just as forward as the flying public. But flight crews don't deserve the stereotyping they sometimes get in this sex-oriented society.

Because I was aware of some of the problems that would face me, from the very beginning of my flying career I was concerned about not breaking communication with the crew. If I did have trouble with them, I knew the words that would put them down in two seconds; I also knew that if I used those words that would be it as far as communication was concerned. So I tried two things that usually worked: humor or pretending ignorance about what they were saying. But sometimes neither worked.

For example, once I was working a night coach flight to San Francisco. It was a long, boring trip since most of the passengers were asleep. I went up to the cockpit to see if the fellows wanted anything to drink, and they were just as bored as we were.

The engineer looked up at me with a smirk and said, "You haven't been up here in some time. I think you're kinda sweet on (and he named my female flying partner who also happened to be my friend). What's the matter, don't you like boys?" Normally I can never think of the right thing to say. This time, however, the words came out before I had a chance to think.

"No. I like 'men.'"

The second officer stared at me, blinked, and said sheepishly, "Oh, yeah."

Passengers, especially, add to the myth of the sexy stewardesses. Although I believe that most of the flying public is now seeing us for who we are—professionals—when I began flying it seemed more fun-and-games to some people. Of course, the "Coffee, Tea, or Me" image was largely generated by the book of the same name, and it fed the fantasies of the already overimaginative public. The problems it created were numerous.

I remember one particular Las Vegas charter. As young and inexperienced as I was, I figured I could handle myself around that bunch of men. They were just like a herd of little boys out for their first fishing trip. It was not unusual to be asked out a half dozen times during the flight. Most of them were wild and woolly . . . and pure talk. But there was one quiet and gentle man who even offered to help us with the meal service. *What a switch,* I thought. *Not even one off-color remark.*

After all the meals were distributed, I sat down on the back jump seat for a minute of rest. My helper came and knelt down on the floor in front of me. Still playing the kindly gentleman, he said, "What color slip do you have on?"

"I beg your pardon?"

"How old are you?"

"Twenty-six."

"Twenty-six years old and a stewardess. Oh, come on now, you've been around!"

Excusing myself, I said crisply, "Sir, you've got the wrong person!"

I also remember the time on a crowded DC-8. I had

YOU CAN FLY! 75

been talking to the people in row 25 when the man sitting in the center seat said, "Where do you all stay on your layover?"

I innocently told him the hotel, and he said, "What's your room number?"

"My room number?" I asked incredulously.

"Come on now," the man said, winking. "I live across the street from some stewardesses. I know how you girls are."

I walked away, stunned.

But the worst insult I've ever received came from a first-class passenger who was a mild-mannered businessman; I even noted his gentle manner as he boarded. Once we were in flight he called me over and handed me a package. I looked at it, thinking at first it was a book of matches. Then I froze as I read the label: it was a package of contraceptives.

He smiled up at me and said, "Just in case you need these."

I handed them back and said, "Sir, I have no use for this."

I walked back to the buffet area, shaking with anger at the insult. I certainly had done nothing to warrant his familiarity. How dare he be so forward with me? I decided this was the time for righteous indignation.

Walking up to his seat again and kneeling down beside it, I spoke quietly but strongly, mincing no words in my explanation to him. The man looked uncomfortable as I told him why I didn't need the contraceptives. I was not rude, and by now I was certainly not embarrassed. He mumbled something about being involved with a church once as I told him of my commitment to Christ. When I returned to the galley area, my anger was a bit mixed with the realization that something he had said to me was probably true: some people *might* have appreciated his "gift."

Of course there *are* two sides to every story. Many people in my profession are living what I consider promiscuous lives. Some do have abortions. Some are alcoholics. But that is typical of the times, *not* of the airline profession as a whole.

Several years ago I had a woman on my flight going to a small city in the Southwest. She was an exquisite woman: well-dressed, soft-spoken, not a blond hair out of place. She was completely at ease traveling, a sophisticated lady in every way.

However, I noticed a vague discontentedness about her as we talked. As the conversation continued, I gained insight into her mood. Her youthful appearance belied her thirty-five years and three broken marriages. Left wealthy by her first husband after they divorced, she had everything she could want materially. At the time we talked, she was on her way to break up with her current boyfriend, one of many in the past few years.

Although I am used to hearing all kinds of honest revelations from passengers, I was not prepared for the frank question she asked me. "Have you ever lived with a man?"

"No, I haven't," I replied.

"Well, you see," she said softly, "I can't live without a man. I have to have someone around."

I believe the greatest lie of Satan to the world and even to the Christian today is, "I have to have someone around."

Since I announced my virginity to the world in the first chapter of this book, you must know that I'm not ashamed of that fact. But it hasn't been easy. For me, the

struggle is not whether or not to hop into bed with someone. The struggle is in dealing with honest human emotions in this sex-crazed generation.

Even as I write this it is hard to know how much to
say, how much not to say. My mind teeters on the tightrope
between compassion and honesty. My head is so full of
other people's hurts and agonies that I weep for them. It's
not necessary to have "been there" to know the horrible
pain in others' lives. More than once a grief-stricken flight
attendant or passenger has poured out his or her sordid story
to me. Then I fall on my knees before God in thankfulness
for what He's kept me from. And it makes me all the more
determined to live a morally pure life.

I didn't set out on a campaign of reforming my co-
workers in the airlines. I never said, "I don't indulge in
sexual promiscuity." I didn't have to. People knew. But I
believe the Christian life is much more than what you don't
do. Being a Christian should be the most positive way of life
in the world!

The story is told of a famous singer who took a group
of friends out to dinner. There wasn't a table available in
the well-known restaurant, so one of the friends leaned
over to the celebrity and whispered, "Why don't you just
tell them who you are?" The older and wiser man whispered
back, "If you have to tell them who you are, you aren't."

After years of coming in contact with more people
than the average person will meet in a lifetime, I know the
impact of living what you believe. Someone has wisely said,
"I'd rather see a sermon than hear one any day." People
need to see us live what we say we believe. Jesus spoke the
words of truth to people . . . but first He got their attention
by His life! Crowds were drawn to Him because He *dared* to
live what He taught. The exciting thing about the Chris-

tian faith is that our Leader, Jesus Christ, not only lived what He taught, but gives us the power to live it too. And as we live our God-given convictions, there is often opportunity to share those beliefs verbally.

I do not believe in sex before marriage. Ever. The Bible is abundantly clear on that. But I am also a human being with needs and desires that are God-given. And, like others, I face today's barrage of off-color remarks, *Playboy* magazines, and attractive men looking for a casual relationship.

Surprisingly, the struggle to survive in today's sex-oriented society is often made harder by Christians. Singles are "fixed-up" by well-meaning friends. We are constantly being told that we need to have "someone around." That, "God has someone special picked out just for you!" I know God intends marriage for most people; but what if, in His sovereignty, He has no special person for me? What if there is *never* any someone? How do I deal with that and not feel short-changed?

Once when two other flight attendants and I were discussing someone's upcoming marriage, one of the women said to me, "Well, Janice, I can't imagine *you* getting married."

Later on the flight that same attendant said to the other woman, who happened to be a close friend of mine, "I think Janice is a virgin."

"She is," replied my friend, "and so was I before I got married."

When my friend told me about the conversation, I approached the other woman and said, "You know, I think sex is great—within marriage. And actually, I'm a very warm person. Why can't you imagine me married?"

"Uh, we'll talk about this later," she hedged.

Of course, we never did. But I thought, *God, what does she think I am—a stick?*

I remember telling Him, "Father, if You wanted to, You could give me the sharpest, best-looking, most spiritual man in the whole world, because You made them all." As I whispered those words to myself and to God, a warm glow of security permeated my whole being. I knew God had the very best for me, with or without a husband.

In rambling through all this maze of confusion, it didn't take me long to realize that I *am* a sexual being. God created me that way. I once heard someone at a health spa say that food is just as bad for you as cigarettes. That's a lie! Food, in the proper amounts, is a good thing. And it is necessary for our survival. Our sexuality is just as vital. Sexuality has to do with who we are as persons: the way we feel about things, our emotions, the way we are made physically. But we have gotten this confused with the sex act. And that's where we get into trouble.

God wants me to relate to others as a whole human being. I am a woman; I am not neuter. I am not ashamed of the emotions He has given me. And because they are so precious, I don't flaunt them. Nor do I have to be preoccupied with thoughts of the sex act. How, then, do I find the balance?

I believe the answer lies in intimacy, and intimacy must start with our Creator, the Lord Jesus Christ.

It might come as a surprise to some people that God knows all about our thought life. He knows about our deep needs and about our desires that can be perverted.

Several months ago I was mentally bombarded with one particular word. I hated the gutter word and everything it stood for, yet it kept entering my thoughts. Panic-stricken, I would confess it and rebuke Satan in the name of

Jesus Christ. I couldn't understand why these dirty thoughts were coming into my mind, and I would cringe in embarrassment when I told God I was sorry.

One day it dawned on me that I was constantly surrounded by the filthy talk of the world. As I walked down the aisle of the plane, my eye would catch sight of the page of a degrading magazine. Or people I was around would spout obscenities. I realized that Satan was the one putting the dirty word in my mind, and he was filling me with guilt for what he had done! So instead of feeling guilty for the word, I just breathed a quick prayer and said, "Father, here it is again. I can't fight the devil, but You can. Take it, Lord." As I determined to think pure thoughts, Satan left me alone.

It helped tremendously to admit my struggles to myself and to God—out loud. As I began to do this, a closeness developed between the Lord and me, a closeness I had never experienced before. As I was honest with God about the intimate things in my life, His love and power began to touch me deeply.

For instance! One night I was home and was rapidly developing a bad case of the blues. Within an hour I was unbearably lonely. My thoughts were consumed with the desire for somebody—a male somebody. I ached with frustration. I cried out to the Lord, "Father, I'm so lonely!"

After a time of weeping and feeling sorry for myself, I said again, out loud, "But, God, I choose You. I know that even if I were married, only You could fulfill my deepest needs." I said this completely in faith, for my emotions said exactly the opposite.

As I repeated those words, a strange thing began to happen. Bible verses I had memorized leaped up at me, and a feeling that I can describe only as overwhelming security swept over me. I was learning to admit my feelings to God and to get His help in handling them. I thought, *This is a turning point in my life.*

Later I talked with a friend who had been happily married for over thirty years. Since I had not told her of my experience with loneliness a few weeks before, I was startled when she said, "You know, sometimes I lie awake at night beside my husband and think, *God, how can I be so lonely?*" I knew then that God had shared something very precious with me. The world is full of people, even Christian people, who are looking for something in their spouses that only God can give them. And I know that without the grace of God I could be one of those people who expect to find in a human being what only Christ can give.

Oswald Chambers said that the things that make God so dear to us are the tiny blessings, because they show His amazing intimacy with us; He knows every detail of our individual lives.

One of the things that makes God so dear to me was revealed recently. Again I was at home alone. I had been thinking about how blessed I was with every possible blessing from God through His faithfulness, not mine. I thought about how much I had learned during the past few years about honesty and communication and taking risks. And I thought about how I was learning to accept myself as God accepted me, warts and all.

My mind wandered to a special couple in my life, both husband and wife are dear friends of mine. And I was thinking especially of his sensitivity to his wife. Many times I had said, "If I could just find a husband like my friend, I would like to get married tomorrow." He seemed to be the most understanding male I had ever known.

Then I thought, *But he doesn't know how a woman*

really feels when she has her monthly period. No man does. Only a woman can know that. A still small voice inside me whispered, "Janice, I know how that feels. I made you." Ideas leaped inside my head as I began to meditate on how God made all of the intimate parts of my body. If He put them together inside of me, surely He does know how I feel at different times of the month. Even if I am overwhelmed by my emotions at times, He isn't. I can trust Him to know what He is doing. I picked up the Bible and read from Psalm 139; the truth and beauty of what I read brought tears to my eyes:

> For you created my inmost being;
>> you knit me together in my mother's womb.
> I praise you because I am fearfully and wonderfully made;
>> your works are wonderful,
> I know that full well.
>
> (Psalm 139:13-14)

The intimacy of that special moment with my Maker brought a whole new realm of understanding with Him.

The other day I flew with a woman who has been married for three years. Her husband is getting his law degree, and right now she is feeling a bit left out of her mate's life. Even though she knows he loves her, he is preoccupied with his studies. She shared this with me, and then she remarked, "Marriage is completely different than I thought it would be." She went on to say that there are two key words that are important as far as she is concerned: communication and consideration.

Later on the same flight, a stew got on to help us as an extra flight attendant. She has been married for ten years and has two children. Her husband is working towards his doctorate in human behavior. She told me, "You know that three-letter word that's supposed to be so important in marriage? Well, it's not nearly as important as everybody thinks! Communication is the word!" Communication *is* the key to *all* good *relationships*, not just marriage.

One of the advantages of being single is having the time to develop relationships with both sexes, and in doing this I'm learning what it means to really communicate. But as much as I love my friends, I know that only my Creator can fulfill my deepest needs. He alone can give me the perfect communication and consideration that no mate, no matter how sensitive, could give me. Because God made me, He not only knows about my needs today, but what my needs will be tomorrow. And He knows facets of my personality that can only be developed by Him. Because He is helping me find the balance, frustration is no longer an overwhelming problem in my life. Oh, I have my moments, as already stated, but I am not repressing or digressing. I am progressing!

One summer several years ago was an unusual summer. From April to September I attended the weddings of six couples and was a participant in two of those ceremonies. As I drove home after the sixth wedding, I smiled with delight as I thought of the happiness of my married friends. My heart was full of joy for them all. As a result of that joy, I began to sing. I sang for thirty minutes before I realized what I was singing; unconsciously the words had become a part of my life:

> I give my heart away
> to the One I love.
> I give my heart away
> to the One I love.
> I give my heart away
> to the One I love.
> Jesus, You're the One I love.

That has become a powerful prayer for me as I struggle to live a pure life for Jesus Christ in my world today. But because I am committed to Him, I can. And I don't have to deny my sexuality. I embrace it!

As I look around at the fast-paced world of today, at the pressure society puts on us all, I want the world to know that everybody is *not* doing it! There are those today who are saying "No" to the world's standards and "Yes" to Jesus Christ. We don't have to give in to the pressures. God has promised us that we can do all things through Him. And all around us are our "balcony people" to cheer us on!

Service Is Being a Servant

You do not do God a favor by serving Him. He honors you by allowing you to serve Him.

Victor Nyquist

"Ma'am, would you like something to drink?" the flight attendant asked. There was no answer. When she repeated her question, the husband glanced up at her and said, "My wife doesn't speak to servants!"

The first time I heard my friend tell about this true encounter she had with a passenger, it made me angry. To put it mildly! I thought of all the grueling hours flight attendants put in. I thought of the varicose veins and kidney problems that sometimes plague the women who fly. I thought of the jet lag and time changes that are an occupational hazard. And I found it difficult to like that woman and her husband. Or even to tolerate them. Fortunately, the incident didn't happen to me. And knowing my friend, she handled it well. But it started me thinking about how I would respond in a situation like that, and it made me question what it means to be a stewardess. Most of all, it made me reexamine what it means to be a servant for Jesus Christ.

My "call" to be a flight attendant was a summons that was just as real to me as if God had spoken audibly. I believed that to be a servant for Him in that way was a high calling. I also knew that being a stewardess meant hard work, and I never expected it to be glamorous. Or did I? When I got the job, I felt I was ready for anything. And I was. Almost.

After a few years of flying I began to notice an increasing pattern among the passengers. While many were polite and grateful for good service, a number of them did not even respond with a "please" or "thank you." Because of my Southern background, this really bothered me. My brothers and I were brought up to respond to people in a mannerly way. Once I remember wanting to be defiant to my mother so I said "Yes" to her instead of "Yes, Ma'am." I never did it again! I realize that this manner of showing respect to elders is a regional custom, but to not say "please" and "thank you" is unheard of. Those words are *not* regional.

As the passengers got ruder and more unresponsive, my attitude changed. I never said anything; I was too "Christian" for that! But I was filled with resentment. I was a servant for Jesus and no one was noticing! It hurt me when somebody failed to express appreciation for what I had done for them.

At first I tried to rationalize the situation. People didn't mean to be that way. Often their harshness was a sign of the turbulent times. But rationalizing didn't soothe my hurt feelings or curb my anger. Finally, I asked God to teach me what I needed to know about being His servant.

One day I was reading Luke 17 in the Living Bible. When I got to the story of the servant, I gulped. I could see myself in the situation as Jesus explained a point to the disciples (vv. 7-8):

> When a servant comes in from plowing or taking care of sheep, he doesn't just sit down and eat, but first prepares his master's meal and serves him his supper before he eats his own.

I thought of the many times I had "come in from plowing" on the airplane. I had answered questions, given out Cokes, and distributed meals for the thousandth time at least. When at last I had a free minute to close the curtain of the buffet area and get a few morsels of food in my own mouth, some passenger would invariably stick his head in and say, "Oh, you eat too?" Sometimes it took all my restraint not to give a sharp reply. What did they think I existed on? Air?

I thought of all those "sheep" I had taken care of in the name of Christ. Sometimes people are so bewildered on an airplane that they have to be taken by the hand and led to the bathroom. I knew that what I was doing was for the glory of God. So why was I feeling so resentful? Tears blurred my eyes as I read the next verses (9-10):

> And he is not even thanked, for he is merely doing what he is supposed to do. Just so, if you merely obey me, you should not consider yourselves worthy of praise. For you have simply done your duty!

"For you have simply done your duty." Those words stung their truth into my soul. I thought of Jesus and the ten lepers. Only one had returned to thank Him. How could I have expected anything more? I must obey God even though I didn't understand the rudeness of people. The rudeness was their problem. Mine was that I had chosen to let them dictate my attitudes and actions. Somebody had to change. And I knew it had to be the one who was determined to obey God! Me.

I began to reexamine my motive for being a flight attendant, thinking back over all my possible reasons for wanting the job. If ever there was the slightest hint of glamour, that was gone. A few months of picking up peas and potatoes off the galley floor had taken care of that!

Perhaps it was the prestige. After all, many girls were dying to be stewardesses, and I had been chosen over hundreds of applicants. But then I remembered the hard time I had had in getting employed by the airlines. And, besides, considering what some people thought of flight attendants, it was no honor! No, I concluded, it was not prestige that made me want to fly.

After days of self-scrutiny, I was left with one motive: I was flying because God wanted me to fly. I still wanted to tell the world about Jesus and His love. I wanted to serve Him and others. But at the same time I realized that somehow I had been trying to do it in my own strength. I had really been thinking, *God is so busy—and I want to help Him all I can!*

It had been many years since my encounter with God in the backyard when I had asked Him to take full control of my life. Had I forgotten that not only did He want me to serve Him, but He had promised to live His life through me? I thought of Galatians 2:20: "I have been crucified with Christ and I no longer live, but Christ lives in me. The life I live in the body, I live by faith in the Son of God, who loved me and gave himself for me."

As I began to understand what being a servant for Jesus Christ really means, life took on a whole new dimension. I began each day with the prayer that I mentioned in the first chapter of this book. "Father, this is (and I say the date). This day has never been except in Your mind. Jesus, live Your life in me today. . . . Lord, *You* are my patience. *You* are my compassion. *You* are my love." I claimed Colossians 1:27: "Christ in you, the hope of glory."

Before when I got irritated, I would pray, "Lord, give me more patience." Or if the person in "seat 34 window" was being unreasonable, I'd say, "Oh, Father, let me love him." Now I saw that my problem was my direction: I was praying *inward* instead of *upward!* Jesus had promised to supply all my needs. And I needed *His* good qualities, not more of my own imperfect ones!

This concept really hit me one night when I was flying with a very senior flight attendant. She was a woman who had trouble with her fellow employees as well as with passengers. In fact, nobody seemed to like her. And, I had to admit, she was a bit strange. But *I* could get along with her! And I enjoyed the fact that though she could be difficult at times, she seemed to respond to me. I even found her challenging.

On this particular flight, I was serving the meals while she poured coffee. As I passed by her with my trays I casually asked, "Would you please serve some coffee to seat 25 aisle?" A natural request. Or so I thought.

With a look that would have put terror into Hitler's heart, she turned to me and snarled, "I'll get it when I get there."

I walked briskly back to the galley, frustration threatening to stifle me as I thought, *Now you know how she is, Janice. Don't let her get to you.* I made it to the privacy of the lavatory just as the tears came.

Anger and hurt feelings poured out with my tears. I thought of all the times this woman had been rude to passengers. I thought of all the times I had covered for her. How could she talk that way to me when I had been so nice to her? Tried to be her friend. How embarrassing that the passengers had heard her rude remark. None of the other crew members even took the time to be nice to her. How dare she treat me that way!

"God, I can't stand her," I sobbed. "She's mean and hateful and I don't like her." I gave one heaving moan of defeat and said, "If You want her loved, You'll just have to do it, because I can't."

"Good," a still, small voice inside me whispered. "I've been waiting for you to say that."

I walked out of the lavatory a few minutes later, dry-eyed and convinced that God's love was tough. He loved that flight attendant just as she was. But I couldn't. Now I was ready to let Him love that ornery character through me. And feelings had nothing at all to do with it. He would show me how to deal with her as I trusted Him.

Geoffrey Grogan has said that understanding can wait but obedience cannot. Many times we don't *do* what God says because we don't understand. Or we take the attitude that He doesn't know what He's talking about. (Of course, we would never *say* that!) It is important to follow God's leading, not only because it is right, but because it is so practical too!

One day while working first class on a DC-8, I encountered an unusual couple. She was blond and petite and oozing with charm. He was dark and rotund and ob-noxious. In fact, his remarks were so bad that the other flight attendant refused to budge from the buffet area. She set up the cart for me while I worked in the cabin. At one point, I was certain we were on "Candid Camera." It must be some kind of joke. Surely no one could talk that way and get away with it for long. Most of his conversation was so absurd. I decided the only recourse was to "kill him with kindness."

As I put the tray table in for his wife and com-mented on her petiteness, he said, "Did you say my wife was fat?"

"Oh, no, sir," I replied. "I said she was petite."

Then as I came down the aisle with a tray of ap-petizers, he snapped "What's this garbage?" On and on it went, insult after insult. God had really given me a zinger this time!

Finally, as the trip neared its end, he stopped me and said, "You know, my wife and I were just talking. You remind us of our niece whom we love very much." I blinked and thanked him. Silently I hoped that he didn't treat his niece the way he had treated me! But I can honestly say I was glad for that difficult encounter. It strengthened my endurance for any similar situations, and God used it to get my attention so I would show special kindness to a sad little man who was alienating everyone around him.

Another thing I learned as a servant was that I must give my resentments to God. For instance, when I was on certain flights, I "resented" people being so demanding. There was one route in particular where this was especially so. Without fail, those passengers would have taken every-thing off the airplane if allowed! And they asked for things nobody else would dream of asking for! Some of their demands could get so unreasonable that it was downright funny. Only at the time I didn't feel like laughing.

My attitude began to change when I saw those passengers through a servant's eyes. Each request became a way of serving my Creator. I also began to see that God *allowed* those people to be unusually demanding.

Every flight attendant has her pet peeve. Mine used to be iced tea! I often work the beverage cart because that gives me more contact with the passengers. I would have my cart loaded with every imaginable beverage. Then someone would order iced tea. And we don't have iced tea, we have to make iced tea. By the glass. From scratch. I wouldn't say anything, but inside I would sigh and think, *Don't they know how much trouble this is going to make?* Of course they didn't! And it wasn't really all that much trouble. The trouble was with my attitude. I expected them to take what I already had set up on the cart. Ice tea took extra effort which I didn't want to make. Soon it became a source of resentment for me.

You may chuckle as you read this. But I'm willing to bet there are "iced tea" resentments in all of our lives. Many times we Christians just won't admit them. How about that husband who likes his eggs cooked just so? Or the wife who wants the tub cleaned *every* time it's used? How about when your parents insist on a curfew that seems absurd to you? Or an employer who doesn't like you wasting time on the job? All reasonable requests. But those little requests can become big resentments if we don't handle them with a servant's heart.

Soon I realized what a big thing I was making out of nothing. And I was losing a golden opportunity to be the willing servant God wanted me to be. Now, I actually love to serve iced tea on the airplane. And I always offer a refill.

For me, it's a little way of going "the extra mile." I am thankful for the iced-tea object lesson God used to teach me a much-needed truth about the Christian life.

As senior flight attendant, I was standing at the door to greet the passengers connecting with our through flight to Atlanta. We had started our trip in Dallas and had two more stops before arriving home. I turned to listen to a man who had just boarded. His voice was filled with sarcasm as he spoke to the woman with him.

"There are no seats in first class, so I suppose that means we have to sit in *second* class?"

I glanced at his boarding pass and walked back into the first-class cabin with him. There were several seats available, and I pointed this out to him. He repeated his question. What he meant was that there weren't two seats *together* in the first-class cabin. I tactfully explained that this was a through flight and people from earlier boarding points had already selected their seats. He created such a scene that a man finally moved to let the two be together.

It has always been important to me that people understand why they can't do something. Sometimes I just need to clear the air too. So before we took off I walked back to explain to the man again why they weren't able to sit together. I thought I was getting through to the couple until the woman looked up at me and said, "Just shut up and go away!"

Startled, I said, "Ma'am?"

"Just shut up!" she said again.

I walked away in shock. Nobody had ever spoken to me that way. I went into the cockpit and closed the door behind me.

The crew's friendly faces turned to greet me. "Hi! How ya doing?" they asked.

I startled all of us by bursting into tears. "That lady back there just told me to shut up," I spluttered.

The copilot started out of his seat. "Where is she? I'll talk with her!"

I assured him that it wasn't necessary—that I would be fine. I just needed to regain my composure. In a few minutes, I headed for the back cabin.

After finishing my work in the tourist section, I still couldn't get the distraught couple off my mind. All I could think of was that it was a misunderstanding, and I wanted it cleared. Maybe they really didn't realize why they couldn't sit together in the first place. And I wanted to make sure that some other stew wouldn't have the same problem with them on some future flight.

Walking up to the couple again, I knelt down beside their seat. I started explaining that it was really important to me that they understand why they couldn't sit together when they first got on the flight. I apologized if I had embarrassed them in any way.

"Well, you did embarrass us," the woman snapped.

I asked how I had done this. She rambled on, not making sense. Her husband didn't say a word, but I could tell he was uncomfortable with his spouse's behavior. Suddenly she looked up at me and again said, "Just shut up!"

Then I finally realized that the lady didn't understand because she didn't want to understand. I could sit there on the floor beside her and talk until Judgment Day and it would do no good. Her mind was made up.

I looked at the man and said, "Thank you, sir." Then I walked away.

I felt a new freedom as I realized that I had done my

best and my responsibility was ended. I was not responsible for their behavior. That lesson about servanthood has proved invaluable to me.

But the beautiful part about being a servant for God is that it doesn't stop there. Jesus tells us that if we do what He commands—be a servant; go the second mile—then we are His friends. "You are my friends if you do what I command" (John 15:14). And in this intimate relationship He tells us things the Father has told Him!

I love the intimacy with the Father described in Psalm 123:2 (NASB):

> Behold, as the eyes of servants *look* to the hand of their master,
> As the eyes of a maid to the hand of her mistress;
> So our eyes *look* to the LORD our God,
> Until He shall be gracious to us.

When you know someone really well, words are not necessary. A look or glance is enough. Who needs to explain what is meant when a mother gives a sharp look to a misbehaving child? Or who can ever put into words the tenderness two lovers exchange as they glance at each other across a crowded room? As we obey God's prompting of servanthood in our everyday life with Him, we will recognize His nod of intimacy in our deepest being.

Robert Browning said that all service ranks the same with God. And the Bible says that God is no respecter of persons. For some that service could mean being the president of a country or a big corporation. For others, it might mean being a housekeeper or a nurse. For me, it's being a flight attendant. And when I'm getting that fifteenth cup of hot chocolate or giving that oxygen demonstration for the five-hundredth time, it helps to know that!

When I began to realize what God has in mind for

me as His servant, eager anticipation replaced burdensome obligation. Dissatisfaction gave way to the joy of knowing the Father's mind. Pleasure replaced drudgery.

"Friendship with God is reserved for those who reverence him. With them alone he shares the secrets of his promises. . . . There is a God in heaven who reveals secrets. . . . I will only reveal myself to those who love me and obey me" (Ps. 25:14; Dan. 2:28; John 14:23).

Although it is painful sometimes, I know that real joy comes from laying down my life for Jesus Christ and for others. I am flying a little higher now as I see servanthood from His perspective!

Communication in a Hurry

Somehow or other, and with the best intentions, we have shown the world the typical Christian in the likeness of a crashing and rather ill-natured bore— and this in the Name of One who assuredly never bored a soul in those thirty-three years during which he passed through the world like a flame.

Dorothy L. Sayers

It was 10:00 P.M. Flight 494 from Atlanta had finally arrived in Tulsa. Bad weather, demanding people, and just plain weariness had taken its toll. My tired brain and body just wanted a clean, warm bed. *How little it takes to make me happy,* I mused.

I quickly gathered my things to exit after my de-planing passengers. As I started up the aisle, I noticed a passenger, Mr. Larsen, coming toward me. As he approached, he opened his arms and embraced me. There were tears in his voice as he spoke. "Oh, God bless you. I'll have to go to my hotel room tonight and weep." And then he walked off the airplane and out of my life. But his pained

99

expression would haunt me for weeks, even months to come when I recalled that awful scene in Atlanta. . . .

It was almost departure time when three people walked on the airplane. Rather, two people half-dragged, half-carried a young girl. At first glance, she looked fine. Then I noticed her glazed eyes and slurred speech. She was obviously on drugs. We notified the captain immediately. After talking with the people, it was obvious they shouldn't be on our flight because of the girl's condition. And after much deliberation between the captain, the agents, and the girl's mother and grandfather, they were asked to de-plane. Yelling obscenities, flailing her arms, and hardly able to stand, the teen-ager was a pathetic picture. Up to this point her companions had been soft-spoken and careful with her. Now, understandably, they became embarrassed and flustered.

"Please be quiet," her mother pleaded.

In exasperation, her grandfather said, "Shut up, just shut up!"

At that, a passenger jumped up from his seat in the rear of the first-class cabin and ran after the three people. His voice trembled with emotion as he yelled, "Don't shout at her. Don't you understand? She needs compassion. Don't talk to her that way!"

I thought, *Nobody would believe this if I told them.* It was like a bad movie. Worse, a nightmare. The kind where you are so relieved to wake up and realize you were only dreaming. But it wasn't a nightmare. It was happening on my flight. Now. And I was in the middle of it.

The girl stumbled down the steps of the plane be-tween her two companions. As she got to the bottom of the stairs, she fell. Immediately, she started having a seizure. Someone yelled for a blanket and pillow. As the small, pitiful body writhed in agony, I ran down the stairs to help. Apparently this had happened before because her mother knew exactly what to do. She quickly thrust a tongue depressor into the girl's mouth to keep her from swallowing her tongue. It was not an epileptic seizure; I had seen several of those before. As I knelt on the cold, hard cement, shielding the girl's eyes from the airplane lights with my body, I shivered. *Lord,* I prayed silently, *tell us what to do.*

Horrible words poured from the girl's mouth. Terror unlike anything I had ever seen darted from her eyes. And rage, like a volcano about to erupt, shook her body. *Oh, God, this must be what hell is like,* I thought. *Father, she's so young.* Tears streamed down my face as I knelt over that frail frame.

But my heart almost broke as I looked in the eyes of the mother. *How many times has she been through this?* I wondered. *Does she ever get used to it? Does it hurt this much every time?*

Eventually, the girl quieted down, and the ambulance came to take her to the hospital. I walked back on the airplane, trying not to appear shaken. But I *was* shaken, and God had not finished with the jolting.

"That man back there is really upset," one of the other flight attendants remarked.

"You mean the one who yelled down the stairs?" I asked. "I'll bet he's had a similar experience with someone in his family."

I walked back to chat with him and learned that the incident we had just witnessed had hit home for our upset passenger, Mr. Larsen. Hard. I listened as he told of his teen-age son being on drugs a few years before.

"The only thing that helped was compassion and understanding," Mr. Larsen concluded.

YOU CAN FLY! 101

"And love?" I asked.

"Yes, and love," he whispered.

Abruptly, he looked at a ring I was wearing. I explained that it was my name written in Hebrew script and that it had come from Israel.

"Are you a born-again Christian?" he asked.

"Yes, I am. And you?"

"I surely am," Mr. Larsen said. His expression was beginning to soften now. The pain seemed to be subsiding a bit. "In fact," he continued, "I came to Christ because of this mess in my family."

A bond formed between us then as Mr. Larsen poured out his heart to me. I felt as if I had known him and his family all my life. And I rejoiced with him as he described the peace God was bringing into their troubled home.

Several times during the flight I had walked up to first class and smiled encouragingly at Mr. Larsen. And he had nodded his head in reply. Other passengers would only remember that grotesque scene, but Mr. Larsen and I would remember something different. I don't think I have ever been so acutely aware of what being a witness for Jesus Christ means as I was on that flight. I was simply available to God.

I wish I could say I have always been that sensitive to the needs and hurts of those around me. I wish I could say I have never botched things up. That I have always done the right thing in showing Christ's love to others in my job. But I wouldn't be honest if I did. I also wouldn't be human. And I am very human!

Invariably the first question asked me after people learn I am a flight attendant and a Christian is, "Do you ever get a chance to witness for Christ in your job?" I always answer in the affirmative and then add, "But it's according to my definition of 'witness.'" Let me explain.

When I committed my life to Christ as a teen-ager, I understood that my life would have to back up my verbal testimony. Later, after entering the airline profession, I quickly learned just how important this was. People would listen to me only if my life was consistent with my words. I took it slow and easy at first. But then I got impatient. I was an evangelical; I was compelled to *tell* people about Jesus Christ. I knew that witnessing for Jesus on an airplane had to be "communication in a hurry." I'd probably never see those people again. And besides, wasn't that my whole reason for being in the airlines?

Eventually, I felt an urgency to share Christ with everyone with whom I came in contact. Now, that's fine if the Holy Spirit is leading you. But I found that many times my "witnessing" was my own idea. Because I am by nature an aggressive person, I would make opportunities when there were none. And I would get depressed if I hadn't gotten a chance to share Christ with someone on the flight. In fact, I felt like a failure!

I had been flying several years before God showed me my problem. He did this through His Word and through loving Christian friends. And because I loved Him and wanted to learn, my heart responded.

Slowly I began to see that it was the Holy Spirit's responsibility to convict and bring people to Christ. My part was to obey God's prompting and let Him do His work through a clean vessel. I asked God to show me what I had been doing wrong in witnessing for Him. When He showed me, it was a painful experience. I had always thought myself sensitive when it came to the feelings of others, so it was distressing to discover that I had often been insensitive.

During this time, a friend impressed upon me the fact that there are different methods of witnessing. Often, if we see someone who isn't sharing like we would, we think they're not really being true to their faith. That's why it is so imperative to be led by the Holy Spirit. God leads each one of us differently.

I remember one particular situation when I had the opportunity to implement what God was teaching me in this area. We were on our way to Phoenix when I spotted a man reading the Bible. After I took his beverage order, I casually remarked, "That's a good book you're reading."

"Yes, it is," he said.

Later, I passed by his seat again and asked, "Are you a Christian?"

"Why, yes," he replied, looking slightly startled.

Encouraged, I continued. "When did you come to know Christ personally?" He seemed flustered as he answered. "Well, my parents were Christians. I've always been a Christian."

Encouraged by his kind face and intrigued by his answer, I sat down by him. I glanced at his Bible. Whole sections were underlined. *Hum, he must know something of the gospel,* I thought.

"Sir, may I see your Bible?" I asked quietly. I began to gently share verses that said we must have a personal encounter with God. The passenger's response was loving and gentle as he listened to me.

In a matter of minutes I realized why the man did not seem to understand what I was saying. I was holding the Book of Mormon! Immediately the Holy Spirit nudged me. "Janice, you can't convince him of the importance of a personal relationship with Christ; only I can do that. Just show him My Word and let Me love him through you."

Later, as we ended our conversation, I said to my Mormon friend, "I believe we both want to know the truth, and God has promised that He will reveal Himself to those who truly want to know Him."

Before, I would have bombarded him with the error of his beliefs. Now, I thanked God for the divine encounter and the opportunity to share His word and show His love.

Sometimes God may want us to share a *word* of witness—just to confess to someone that we're a Christian. When I learned this, I cringed as I remembered the times when someone had shown an interest in spiritual things and I had bombarded them with the whole plan of salvation!

A friend of mine once had a well-known astrologer on her flight. "Suddenly," she recalled, "I knew God wanted me to go up and just tell that woman I was a Christian." In a natural and loving way, the flight attendant went up and introduced herself to the woman and her traveling companion. In the course of the conversation, she was able to tell them she was a Christian. At that, the astrologer's companion turned to my friend and asked about her relationship to God. For several minutes there was an opportunity to share about the living Christ with both passengers. And all because my friend obeyed the Lord.

When I learned to relax and let Jesus live His life through me, all the pressure of *having* to share Christ was off. God knew the intent of my heart; I didn't have to worry if I was being an effective witness for Him. What a big lesson for this zealous evangelical! And I'm still learning.

After I put up that sign in the stewardess lounge, something happened which I never expected. My co-workers would sometimes come to me and tell me that "so and so claims to be a Christian, but let me tell you what she did." I began to feel the burden of every Christian flight attendant in the airlines. I knew it was important that we live an effective life for Christ in our jobs. Some people we work with have had Christianity crammed down their throats in earlier years. They desperately need to see a supernatural God at work today. My heart grew heavy with the negative reports. It took all my commitment to live my own life. How could I possibly straighten out everybody else?

Gradually, however, I realized that the stories I was hearing might not even be true. Usually the person reporting did not even claim to be a believer. She was relating things through *her* eyes. I decided to give my sisters in Christ the benefit of the doubt until I knew for a fact that something was true. And when they were true, I had to understand that my struggling sisters (and brothers) had their difficult times, just as I still had mine.

Airline people are impressed by good manners. They don't care how many books you've written or how wealthy you are or what your position might be. The only thing that leaves a good, lasting impression is courtesy. The first question that is asked when someone mentions having a well-known person on board is: "Was he (or she) nice?" I think about a Christian celebrity whose rude, obnoxious behavior is well-known among flight attendants. What a denial to the Christ life!

I remember well a flight to the West Coast a few years ago. As I walked down the aisle with a tray of champagne, my eyes caught the title of a Christian book a woman was reading. I asked if she wanted some champagne, and she put down the book, smiled sweetly, and said, "No, thank you."

I asked her husband sitting beside her, and he growled, "I'll have a Coke." I explained that the attendant behind me was coming with other beverages.

Looking over at the woman, I asked, "Isn't that book published by Tyndale House? I've been wanting to read it."

With that her husband looked up at me with interest. "And how would *you* know about Tyndale House?"

"Because I'm a Christian. You are, too, aren't you?"

The passenger's attitude changed completely. He and his wife responded warmly to me as we briefly shared our mutual faith in Christ. Later, when the other stew who had served his Coke mentioned his changed attitude, we both couldn't help but wonder what would have happened if we hadn't been Christians. What if the Holy Spirit had told the man to witness to us as unbelievers? We both agreed that he wouldn't have gotten our attention because of his rudeness.

Once a man came on my flight wearing a cross in his lapel. He had on a dark suit and a scowl to match. Although I talked with him, there was no warmth, no joy in knowing Jesus. Of course, he could have been having a bad day. But what about a few weeks later when he flew with us again and the same thing happened? Another bad day?

Sometimes we Christians forget how we look through the eyes of the world.

One day a passenger and I were having a good conversation. Finally I commented on his dove pin. "Are you a Christian?" I asked.

"Yes, I am," he replied. "Are you?"

When I said yes, he suddenly asked, "Have you been baptized with the Holy Spirit?"

"Yes, I have," I replied. "But I don't have the gift of tongues." I had anticipated his next question.

"Oh, you're got a lot in store," he said. Abruptly, he queried, "Do you know any Scripture songs?"

"Why, yes, I do."

"Sing some of them for me."

"Well, I don't think this is the place right now." I felt as if this man was testing me to see if my Christian experience was real. I excused myself and went back to my flight duties.

As I thought about the incident, the Lord impressed me with the fact that I had done the same thing to others. I had "interrogated" people in the same manner. Because of my evangelical background, it was important to me that people use the "right words"; that they explain themselves in a way that was satisfactory to *me*. And if they didn't talk or act as I thought they should, I would put them in a certain category. *Liberal*, I would think. Or *not getting the right teaching*. I didn't understand that though people don't always know the "right" words to say, their experience with Jesus Christ is no less valid than mine.

Because I longed to fly even higher with Him, I wanted God to teach me. But sometimes He had to get my attention in unique and painful ways.

When I heard those negative stories about airline personnel or passengers who were Christians, I knew God was telling me to reexamine myself. Was my attitude right? Was I harboring resentful thoughts? After all, didn't Jesus say, "Let he who is without sin cast the first stone" (see John 8:7)? Every incident I heard about, every Christian I encountered, gave me the opportunity to look at my own heart.

108

I also decided that God might be trying to tell me something about the involved person and that this was His way of getting me to pray for that person. So I began to ask Him to let me see that negative situation through His eyes and even thanked Him for getting my attention that way. (Although sometimes I didn't feel very thankful!)

Not long ago, an attractive woman was on my flight. She was in her sixties, beautifully dressed. But what I really noticed was her graciousness. I found myself making excuses to go by her seat and have little half-minute chats.

On that same flight was a woman who wore a "Jesus First" pin. She was not rude, but she was also not smiling or even pleasant. I thought, *How sad.*

I noticed that my "gracious" lady was reading a Christian book. When I expressed an interest in what she was reading, she said, "I thought you were one."

"You're very observant," I remarked. I had no idea how she knew I was a Christian, but she did.

"I try to be aware," she replied.

I knelt beside her and asked how long she had known the Lord. "For twenty-four years," she said. "Before that I was an alcoholic." She told me she traveled all over telling people about Christ. Now I was even more captivated by her warmth.

Suddenly I found myself telling her about the "Jesus First" lady. Then my new-found friend gave me some advice that confirmed what the Lord was teaching me.

"That's where she is in her Christian life," said the wise lady. "She's not manifesting the fruit of the Spirit right now. We are to be discerning; but we're not to judge."

As I encounter all sorts of people every day, I'm learning to stop and ask God to let me see that situation through *His* eyes. Sometimes I've learned truths about myself from seeing another person's mistakes. I'm growing, but I might not have had the courage or the desire to change if God had not gotten my attention through another's life.

"Do you get many chances to witness for Christ on the airlines?" you still may be asking. Let me answer you by quoting some of my favorite lines:

I will exalt you, my God the King;
  I will praise your name for ever and ever.
Every day I will praise you
  and extol your name for ever and ever. . . .
  and I will proclaim your great deeds . . .
  celebrate your abundant goodness
  and joyfully sing of your righteousness.

(Ps. 145:1-2, 6-7)

It's not a question of "do I witness?" When my life is cleansed and His Spirit is leading me, *I can't help but tell of His greatness.* And it is so natural and so right that afterward I am awed that He could ever use me at all.

The Downdrafts

If we could see the floor of God's immediate presence
we would find it strewn with the 'toys' of God's
children who have said . . . this is broken, I can't
play with it any more, please give me another pre-
sent. Only one in a thousand sits down in the midst
of it all and says . . . I will watch my Father mend
this.

Oswald Chambers

I remember the first time I was ever in severe turbulent weather. Pillows flew out of the overhead rack. Soft drinks fell out of their storage compartments and rolled down the aisle. People groaned with air sickness. We were all shaken clear through to our bones.

But the worst part of turbulence is the downdraft. When an airplane hits this, it can drop as much as several thousand feet in seconds. If you're not buckled in, you'll fly up toward the ceiling while the airplane appears to remain stable.

One of the interesting side effects of my first experience with severe turbulence was a feeling of helplessness.

As the weather got progressively worse, I thought, *This is it!* We were bumped and shaken and rattled so much that my only thought was *If anything happens to me, mother will have to pay all my bills.* Then I thought, *You dummy, you've got all that insurance. It's more than enough to pay your bills!* An eerie sort of peace came over me. I was resigned to the fact that my life might soon be over. Obviously it wasn't the end, and after I got on the ground, the initial fear left. But that intense sense of helplessness and hopelessness stayed with me for a long time.

As I thought about this later, it seemed God had a lesson in it for me. When I put my faith and trust in people rather than Him, it can produce that same feeling of helplessness. And just as the weather seemed to control the airplane, other people seem to control my feelings at times.

Downdrafts are caused by variations in air temperature; the variations of behavior in other people can cause deep disappointment. Many times we expect others to be the stabilizing force in our life that only God can be. We have all been shaken and rattled and bumped by the attitudes and actions of others, because people blow hot and cold just like the air. And that kind of turbulence can send us into a tizzy.

My own spiritual struggle in this area began several years ago when I finally realized the high expectations I had for other people as well as myself. This dawned on me when my friend Martha said one day, "Whatever they do, it's never enough, is it, Jan?" I was humiliated that she had hit so close to home. But that statement forced me to start growing in an area of my life that I had never had the courage to recognize before.

King David learned this lesson the hard way. He mentions it over and over in the Psalms: He knew that only

Jehovah God could fulfill his deepest expectations. And my heart began to cry with David as I confessed to the Lord: "Find rest, O my soul, in God alone; my hope comes from him" (Ps. 62:5). I was beginning to see how I had trusted in people for what only my Creator could do.

This lesson was learned over and over as God brought people and situations into my life to test me. The habit of expecting too much of others had taken a lifetime to form. It would not be broken overnight.

I was always disappointed when people didn't respond the way I wanted them to respond. If I shared something that was exciting to me and others didn't rejoice the way I did, deep down I would be hurt.

Just last year the Lord really worked in my heart regarding this problem. He began when I attended a counseling seminar in my church every Monday night for three months. (Like most Christians these days, I've been to almost every seminar, workshop, or lecture that is offered on the evangelical market.) At this particular series of classes, I saw with blinding clarity that I had not been allowing Jesus Christ to meet my needs of security and significance. I saw how, with alarming regularity, I was unconsciously trying to let other people meet that need. Consequently, I was always disappointed.

I am by nature very outgoing and positive. To admit that anyone had hurt me would be "negative." There was enough negativism around me, and I wanted no part of that. Besides, I knew the Christian life was to be a victorious one, and I wanted to show victory in every area of my life. Thus, I had built up an impossible situation for others. No human being in the world could come up to the standards I had set for them.

Several years ago a person whom I loved and respected disappointed me deeply. She was someone who had a strong influence on my spiritual life. I had learned many truths from God's Word through this friend. As a result, I put her on a spiritual pedestal. Eventually, through a series of circumstances, she disappointed me deeply and hurt many other people as well. What disturbed me most was that my friend did not seem to understand that her actions affected so many. But what I didn't see at the time was *my* negative feeling toward her. What started out as disappointment turned to grief. Then grief turned to anger. And anger turned to hate. Eventually I could not bear to be around her. Appalled at my intense feelings, I thought, *This is not like me. I've never felt hate for anyone in my life. What's wrong with me?*

Slowly God began working in my heart and I began dealing with the situation. Over the course of a year, I recognized and understood some deep truths about human nature. Oswald Chambers puts it this way:

> Many of the cruel things in life spring from the fact that we suffer from illusions. We are not true to one another as facts; we are true only to our ideas of one another. Everything is either delightful and fine, or mean and dastardly, according to our idea.

Was that what I had been doing? Dealing with "illusions"? I thought of my friend. Yes, she *had* hurt me deeply. But what had I done to her? All I could see was *my* hurt. What about hers? I had put her in an impossible situation. I loved her and respected her deeply, but I had never allowed her to fail. To be a human being. Unconsciously I had wanted her to be for me spiritually what only God can be. No one can measure up to that. While she was responsible for any wrong she had done, *I* was responsible for my actions and my attitude toward her.

Chambers goes on to say:

Our Lord trusted no man, yet He was never suspicious, never bitter. Our Lord's confidence in God and in what His grace could do for any man was so perfect that He despaired of no one. If our trust is placed in human beings, we shall end in despairing of everyone.

Shortly after all this hit me, I was sharing a bit of news with someone close to me. I knew she was not really hearing what I was saying, so I paused and said, "Well, what do you think?" Her response showed she had completely missed my point. As I looked at her, I thought, *She will never understand the way I want her to understand, and it's all right.* I was able to accept her just as she was.

The sense of release I experienced touched me so deeply that I wept later as I shared this incident with my counseling instructor.

"At last I see that Jesus Christ is my only source of security and significance. But why has it taken me so long to learn this?" Then I sputtered out the underlying issue that had been bothering me: "I was supposed to know all that!"

His kind, reassuring response warmed my heart. In fact, it helped give me the courage to make some changes in my life that God had been speaking to me about for a long time. I had never realized before how much it mattered to me what people thought of me, especially those nearest and dearest. I was at last learning to let God be God and people be the frail human beings that we all are.

But I was much easier on other people than I was on myself. My idealistic expectations of Janice were harder to learn to live with. God taught me in a way that I never would have chosen.

Through an incident I am not free to share, I disappointed a person very much. Unintentionally, I broke her heart. But her disappointment in me seemed dwarfed by my disappointment in myself. I had always thought of myself as being very sensitive to the feelings of others. To discover my own carelessness threatened to undo all the growth potential I had experienced. But God in His mercy showed me that I, too, am a finite human being. I can disappoint others, just as they can disappoint me.

I have always had a deep love for people. Even before I became a Christian, I delighted in the company of others. As I have already shared, I am a "people" person, not an academic soul. I have always had an insatiable desire to know people and have them know me. As a teen-ager I read a book by Normal Vincent Peale called *Stay Alive All Your Life*. That book changed my life. In it, the author said a great deal about enthusiasm and openness and loving people. As a result, I deliberately chose, at nineteen, to be a transparent person. Somehow I knew it might cost me something, but I never realized how *much* it might cost.

After going through the difficult process of getting my job and even the traumatic cheating incident, I still chose to be open and honest and as genuine as I knew how. I worked hard at listening and caring about people. And I was determined to be sensitive at any cost. Any book or lecture on relationships attracted me. I truly believed God was making me into His sensitive woman. And even though now I have been shaken and rattled and thrown by the turbulence of disappointment in others as well as myself, I still want to be God's sensitive woman. And that involves having my expectations in Him, not in people. Those expectations have caused a lot of suffering sometimes. God forbid that suffering be in vain.

Sometimes it is hurtful to grow in the ways of God. But growth never comes without some form of struggle or pain. We are all delicate creatures. Rather like that emerging butterfly perhaps.

I am trying not to expect so much from others, and most of the time I succeed. With myself, it is a bit harder. But I am learning that though I make mistakes, though I sin, God forgives me. I am even able to laugh at some of my blunders. And weep.

Not long ago I came across a statement that beautifully expresses the thoughts of my heart.

> If suffering is accepted and lived through, not fought against and refused, then it is completed and becomes transmuted. It is absorbed, and having accomplished its work, it ceases to exist as suffering and becomes part of our growing self.

Fear . . .
Friend or Foe?

*The adventurous life is not one exempt from fear,
but on the contrary one that is lived in full knowledge
of fears of all kinds, one in which we go forward in
spite of our fears.*

Paul Tournier

I have always been afraid of deep water. Although I
can swim enough to keep from drowning, that liquid stuff
has never appealed to me. This is ironic since I lived near
the ocean for most of my childhood and teen-age years. But
when we went to the beach, I was always the one who built
sand castles and looked for sea shells. No splashing around
for me! I wanted to be "safe."

Several years ago when my airline was awarded the
route to London, I got excited about flying there. Until I
found out I had to be "over water qualified" to do it. That
meant training with a life raft and jumping into deep water.
Was I brave enough?

119

My sense of adventure finally won out, and I applied for special training, trying not to think about the day when we would practice with the inflated life raft in the water.

But the day did come! There we were—gathered around the pool in our life vests. The two male instructors were kind but firm. *Everyone* had to go through all of the procedures to be FAA qualified. I swallowed hard as I thought about jumping off the diving board into the water. I had never jumped off a diving board in my life! I began to question my sanity. *Let somebody else fly to London,* I thought.

I felt a little better when they divided us into two groups: swimmers and non-swimmers. I gladly went with the novices and sighed with relief that I wasn't the only one.

Down at the shallow end of the pool I glanced around at the others. They didn't look so fearful. Why should I? I sneaked a peek at our instructor, then chuckled to myself. Maybe I wasn't so dumb after all. *We* had gotten the best-looking one!

The first thing our blond Adonis told us to do was submerge our bodies in the water. I came up sputtering. I also came up with stinging, burning eyes. I had forgotten that my eye make-up was not waterproof! As I rubbed them, they got worse. Finally I yelled for help. Exit pride. I was more concerned about survival than appearance.

After I learned that it was perfectly safe to be in the water with a life vest on, I found I could float easily. *This might not be so bad.* I concluded. Then the other instructor yelled for us to come down and join the swimmers. My day of reckoning had come!

I stood by the pool, still scared, but knowing I must finish what I had started. If this was what I had to do to get qualified to fly to London, by George, I'd do it! But my heart almost skipped a beat when I heard our tutor say, "Now I want each of you girls to jump off the side of this pool before we go to the diving board." He had to be kidding! It was going to take every ounce of my courage to do the diving board bit; I hadn't counted on the side of the pool thing!

I lined up to jump. The quicker the better. I breathed a sigh of relief when I saw the instructor a few feet out in the water waiting to pull us up. It no longer mattered to me that he was cute or had a good build. He was a life-guard! Closing my eyes, I plunged. My kind coach grabbed me; he knew I was scared.

Later someone laughingly said, "You jumped right into his arms!"

"That was the idea," I said, "but not for the reason you think!"

Eventually, I did my first diving board jump, and even though I was terrified, I made it. By the end of the day I was so sore from pushing and pulling and getting in and out of the water I thought I had been in a battle. But it was a battle I had won. Not without fear, of course, but the victory was mine. My reward came when one of the other stews congratulated me.

"I know you're afraid of the water," she said. "I admire you for what you did."

Fear can *motivate*. When you want to do something badly enough, you can usually do it. Fear is overcome by the desire to do the thing. History gives countless examples of people who overcame deep fear to accomplish their dreams and goals. Christ was one. Christ, the man, experienced fear when He prayed with fervor: "My Father, if it is possible, may this cup be taken from me" (Matt. 26:39).

But that fear was overcome by His greater motivation to do the will of the Father. That Jesus chose to live beyond His emotions was clearly evidenced in the conclusion of His prayer: "Yet not as I will, but as you will." And His actions that followed changed the course of history as well as millions of lives.

Most of us have such deep-seated and ingrained fears that we actually believe we can never overcome them. And even though we are committed Christians and believe God's Word, we may have a hard time really experiencing that Word when it says: "In all these things we are more than conquerors through him who loved us" (Rom. 8:37). In this case, fear can *manipulate*.

Fear chained me in the prison of self-doubt for years. You know of my failure in high school, my subsequent cheating in stew school, and eventually how my conscience was cleared. "And she lived happily ever after," the stories usually go. Well, yes . . . and no!

When I walked out of the training center that afternoon years ago after confessing to my instructor, I felt like a brand-new person. But deep inside lurked the fear that possibly I would not have made it as a stewardess if I had not cheated. I knew where that feeling came from: the Bible tells us that Satan is the father of lies. But *that's how I felt*. The next time I went to recurrent training, which is held every year and which every flight attendant must attend, and the overwhelming feelings of self-doubt came up again, I did sneak a couple of glances at another person's paper. Horrors! "You did that . . . *again?*" Yes, again. And within two seconds I was mortified at what I had done. Later, I asked forgiveness.

My feelings of inadequacy and failure were so deep that I actually felt insecure in that area even though I knew

I was basically as capable as everyone else. For several years I was not able to go to training and take a test without getting emotionally torn up about it. Finally one year I got desperate and decided to ask God to help me.

Several years ago, my company acquired a new fleet of airplanes and every flight attendant had to qualify to do flight duty on these jets. As soon as I heard the news, my stomach started fluttering. The night before the training, I realized how desperately tired I was of being scared of tests all the time. I knew I could learn just like everyone else. I knew the other attendants dreaded these training days; and I knew some were just as nervous as I was about taking tests. But I also knew I wanted God to deliver me from this inordinate fear.

As usual, my help came from God's Word. As I was reading through the Psalms, I prayed, "Lord, I'm sick of this fear. Please give me something that will apply to me personally in this situation." Immediately my eyes fell on a verse; I knew it was the one I was to take as my own for the next day's training. "When my anxious thoughts multiply within me, Thy consolations delight my soul" (Ps. 94:19 NASB). I began to meditate on that verse. What I learned that night became riveted to my heart and eventually quelled my fear.

"*When* my anxious thoughts" . . . that told me anxious thoughts would come. I was not unique in my anxiety. I might be fearful of failure—a natural emotion considering my past record—but everyone has fears. Although it is hard for me to comprehend, some folks are afraid to fly. Others are fearful of financial failure. Still others are apprehensive of elevators, or cats, or whatever. Everyone, at one time or another, fears something.

"When my anxious thoughts *multiply* within

YOU CAN FLY!   123

me. . . ." Remember that potato chip commercial, "Bet you can't eat just one"? God showed me that if those anxious thoughts aren't handled quickly and in the right way, they multiply.

One day I was driving home from a friend's house. We had had a great time of fellowship and prayer. But while we were praying, the thought came to me, *What if my mother died?* Instead of having a healthy attitude about this, I began to dwell on it. In fact, I got very morbid, imagining all kinds of horrible details. By the time I got home, my mother was dead and buried and I was overwrought with worry! I soon realized what had happened and immediately confessed it to the Lord. I had allowed that one thought, a perfectly natural one, to *multiply* within my mind. Someday, my mother will actually go to be with Him; but I am not to be preoccupied with that until, in His timing, He allows it. And maybe we'll just go up to heaven together!

But that verse says something else that caps it all for me: "When my anxious thoughts multiply within me, *Thy consolations delight my soul.*" What does it mean to have God delight my soul? Another verse in the Psalms is the very picture of being consoled by God. It is Psalm 131:2 (NASB): "Like a weaned child *rests* against his mother, my soul is like a weaned child within me." In my mind's eye, my soul is resting on my Father, Mother, Husband, Rock—Jesus Christ, Jehovah God. And sometimes He allows fears to drive me there. I think of the words of George MacDonald:

> What if God knows prayer to be the thing we need first and most? What if the main object of prayer is the supplying of our need—our endless need—the need of Himself? Hunger may drive the runaway child home, and he may or may not be fed at once, but he needs his mother more than his dinner.

Communion with God is the one need of the soul beyond all other need—prayer is the beginning of that communion, and some need is the motive of that prayer. So begins a communion, a talking with God, a coming to one with Him, which is the sole end of prayer, yea of existence itself in its infinite phase. We must ask that we may receive, but that we should receive what we ask in respect to our lower needs is not God's end in making us pray. To bring His child to His knee, God withholds that man may ask.

Is that what God was doing in allowing my fear of tests to continue? Was it true that all I had to do was come to Him and be consoled by His Word? I thought of an incident when I had desperately needed His consolation.

In all my years of flying, I had never had anyone die on my flight. Oh, I had given oxygen many times and had had my share of emergencies. Once a lady had hemorrhaged and been near death, but we made an unscheduled landing and rushed her to the hospital. But I had never had anyone die. Then one day it happened.

It had been a pleasant three-day trip. I enjoyed flying with the other three girls; they were efficient, courteous, and professional in every way. We were on our last day, about to finish up, when we walked into the gatehouse at Miami International to board our flight. I glanced around the waiting area and noticed a pitiful-looking woman slumped down in a wheelchair. Two companions were standing beside her, trying to get her straightened in the chair. I went over to see if I could help. When I touched her, she was as cold as ice. Her friends told me she was transferring from one nursing home to the other; they were waiting for a nurse to come in from Detroit to accompany the woman on her flight. A warning signal went off in my head then. I didn't see how she could make the trip.

Later, when the crew boarded the plane to do their usual preflight duties, I walked up to the cockpit to introduce myself to them. One of the other girls I had been flying with was chatting with them.

"Hi. I'm Janice."

"Oh, ho ho! We've heard about you," said the captain. "My name is Jesus."

"Yeah, and God is my copilot," heckled the first officer.

I blinked, not believing what I was hearing. I had never met these men before. What had brought this on? What had my flying partner been telling? I looked straight at them, decided to ignore the rude remarks, and asked, "Okay, fellows, can I get you something to drink?"

As I walked out the cockpit door, my mind was reeling. I shot up a quick prayer to God: "Lord, I don't know what's going on. As far as I know, I've done nothing to merit this. And I thank You for being persecuted for Jesus' sake. And, Lord . . . I'm going to 'kill them with kindness!' "

Earlier that morning I had prayed my usual prayer and had specifically thanked God for whatever He would bring into my life that day. I knew He was the God of all circumstances, that things didn't "just happen." But I certainly had not counted on something like this! A strange calm swept over me as I realized God had allowed those men to talk to me like that. And I thanked Him for helping me not to react to their insensitivity. Above all, I felt wonderfully consoled by Him. It was almost as if He were there beside me saying, "Just wait, Janice, this flight's not over yet. Watch and see what happens."

We had been in the air about ten minutes when the seat belt sign went off, and my partner and I got up to prepare our first-class service. About that time, one of the attendants came up from tourist with an oxygen bottle. Because I was senior flight attendant, she approached me asking for assistance. It was for the woman I had encountered in the waiting area. When we put the oxygen bottle on her, I knew she was already dead. The nurse sitting beside her nodded her confirmation. Rushing up front, I picked up the PA to ask if there was a doctor on board. Then I called the crew.

"We have a lady on board who has just died."

"What?" Their immediate reaction was one of disbelief.

"I've called for a doctor on board. I'll talk with you in a few minutes."

"We'll call the company immediately." No heckling this time! We were a team now, desperately wanting to do the right thing.

Several hours later, we landed in Detroit, our original destination. Usually, we would make an emergency stop. But in this situation, it was decided by the company via radio to continue to our destination. The lady was deceased, although that was not official until a coroner in Detroit pronounced it. There was nothing that could be done for her, and her daughter was waiting for her in Detroit.

Later, after what seemed like endless reams of paperwork done by the captain and myself, we were allowed to go to the hotel to rest. I approached him and thanked him for his thoughtful, professional attitude and actions during the whole situation. He smiled at me and said, "Look, thank you. You were great."

As I went up to my room, I could hardly keep back the tears after that long, emotion-packed day. I had seen a

YOU CAN FLY! 127

human being die; it was a sobering thing. But most of all, I had been consoled by God. He had drawn me to Himself in an unusual way because of the vileness of men. And that consolation was brought home to me as I thought, *Father, I bet the next time that crew hears the name Janice Barfield or Christian they'll think something different!* Because I had turned the crews' heckling over to Him, despite my confused feelings, He had rewarded me with His peace. I was overwhelmed at His gift of love and consolation.

We've seen how fear can *motivate, manipulate,* and *multiply.* But there is also a good fear, a healthy fear, a fear sadly lacking in most of us. David, along with others in the Bible, knew it well. It is the fear of God. And the Scriptures define it as a holy, reverential awe of God. When we fear Him with all our hearts, it puts every other fear in the right perspective. This fear can *maintain* a right relationship with God.

We are living in a treacherous world today. Never in history has humanity had the power to destroy itself with the touch of a finger. Lawlessness is rampant. Some people would just as soon shoot you as look at you. The crazy and bizarre have become everyday occurrences.

What, then, are we to do? Live in fear, like the rest of the world? Afraid to leave our homes because of what may happen? No! The Bible tells us this is the very time we are to focus our fear on God—to trust in Him. And the worse things get, the greater our opportunity to fear Him! *He* is our fortress, *He* is our deliverer, *He* is our strong right arm. The key to overcoming the wrong kind of fear is focus. Focus on Jehovah, the object of our faith.

Sometimes people ask me if I'm afraid to fly. When I was younger, I always said, "No." As I have gotten older, there have been times when I have been afraid. Sitting by the entrance of the DC-9 with hailstones thumping outside the door can bring that fear. But it is fleeting. For I am learning to commit each fear to the One of whom David said, "But I trust in you, O Lord; I say, 'You are my God.' My times are in your hands" (Ps. 31:14-15). And I am reminded of the words of that precious old hymn, "Amazing Grace":

> Through many dangers, toils and snares,
> I have already come;
> 'Tis grace hath brought me safe thus far,
> And grace will lead me home.

As I fear God, each inordinate fear becomes a way of getting closer to Him.

John A. Shedd said, "A ship in the harbor is safe—but that is not what ships are for." It is not always *safe* to be a Christian in our world today. Sometimes it is a fearful thing. I think of my younger days as a teen-ager, when I was oblivious to fear. I was free and idealistic and loved Jesus with all my heart. It never occurred to me to be afraid. I had Him, and together we could do anything! But as the years passed, fears crept in. Sometimes these fears overcame me, and I was almost drowned with defeat. Some of those fears stayed with me a long time. And just when I began to fly spiritually with Him, loving every moment of the beautiful view, some old gnawing habit would creep back in until I felt like retreating back into that cocoon again. But somehow, deep inside, there was still the desire to risk, to be challenged, to not be "safe."

We Christians don't talk about our fears very much. In my group, especially, we talk about the "victorious life." And I believe in that victorious life with all my heart! In fact, I am experiencing that life in many ways. But that

YOU CAN FLY! 129

doesn't mean all the struggles are over. Sometimes I'm scared. I still have fears. But, He is helping me. And someday, praise God, there won't be any more fears!

In the meantime, I choose to go on despite those apprehensions. Because I am a human being, those fears will come. But I know who I fear more! And I long to go where He goes, my Fear-Bearer, my Battle-Fighter, my Victor!

> He chose a street
> where he wouldn't be safe
> and nobody there would save him.
>
> He went to the parties
> that were not safe
> not saying who, but they knew him.
>
> He went down the road
> to the Place of the Skull.
> The soldier was there, and the criminal,
> and the ones who thought if he didn't have pull
> they wouldn't be safe to know him.
>
> He couldn't be safe
> and come where we
> go, and hide,
> and storm, and agree
> on everything else if only he
> wouldn't show up our artful way
> with the light of his simplicity.
>
> No. He couldn't be safe and be
> our Savior.

Knowing the truth of these words helps prepare me for the days ahead. That truth makes all the struggle of the past . . . and the future . . . worthwhile!

Before I
Take Off . . .
Again

Forward! Thy orders are given in secret. May I
always hear them—and obey. Forward! Whatever
distance I have covered, it does not give me the right
to halt. Forward! It is the attention given to the last
steps before the summit which decides the value of all
that went before.

Dag Hammarskjöld
Markings

One day a girl went out to Heathrow Airport near London, England, just to share Christ with the passengers as they walked by. She came upon a stewardess who was receptive; in fact, the stewardess made a commitment to Christ just as her flight was being called. Rummaging through her bag, the girl looked for something for the stew to take with her. All she had was a book by Francis Schaeffer. The woman gladly took it and hurried to meet her flight.

Standing there watching that stew disappear among the hundreds of people, the Good-News bearer silently prayed for God to send someone on the flight to tell her more about Jesus Christ.

Later, the stew wrote the girl and told her what had happened on the transatlantic trip.

She had finished her flight duties and was sitting on the jump seat flipping through the book given to her. Suddenly a passenger walked up and asked, "What do you think of that book you're reading?"

"Well, I really can't understand it," she replied. "You see, I've only been a Christian a few hours."

The man looked down at her kindly and said, "Perhaps I can help you. My name is Francis Schaeffer."

I love that story. It shows what kind of God we have. And far from being extraordinary, I believe that stories like that should be a part of the lives of everyone who claims to know Jesus Christ in a personal way.

I am one ordinary woman, but I have an extraordinary God. When I committed my life to Him at thirteen, I did so with every fiber of my being. I was so young and so idealistic I didn't have any more sense than to take Him at His word! Many of my ideals were false and were shattered, as you saw; but He is taking them and, as the song goes, "making something beautiful" of them.

To me, the Christian life can be compared to a duty that I must have done *at least* ten thousand times in my seventeen years of flying. Remember how the stewardess always holds out her tray when she asks you if you want coffee? More times than I can tell, people will say, "Oh no, I don't want cream or sugar, just give me coffee."

"Ma'am, just give me your cup."

"But I don't want anything in it. Just coffee."

"Ma'am, please, your cup."

Finally, it will get through to them: if they want their coffee, they'll have to cooperate and give the stew their cup. Then they get what they wanted in the first place.

132

When we commit our lives to Christ, we are excited. But somehow, along the way, we forget to give ourselves to Him so He can fill us up with *His* good things. We often spend our days protesting, "God, I don't want that."

"Give Me your cup."

"Lord, You didn't make *him* go through that. Why me?"

"Give Me your cup."

"Jesus, this is too hard. I can't do it."

"Give Me your cup."

"Oh, Father, You've ruined my life now. How can I ever get over this?"

"Give Me your cup."

And God, who is so loving and so long-suffering, waits for us to cooperate and give Him our lives. He wants to fill us up with Himself.

Oswald Chambers said, "Never make a principle out of your experience; let God be as original with other people as He is with you."

As you have read through these pages, I hope you have seen beyond Janice Barfield and her experiences. I hope you have seen God in a new way. And I hope you have realized how very special *you* are to Him. God works in each person's life in a different way. My experiences are not yours, and yours are not mine. Each of us is unique.

And God doesn't care if you've been a Christian two weeks and are just trying to make sense of your commitment or if you've known Him from age seven; He wants to take you out of that cocoon and strengthen you for the flight ahead. And when you turn every experience, both good and bad, over to Him, He will dazzle the eyes of the world with the brilliance of your colors!

YOU CAN FLY! 133

In these exciting days, may we who bear His name walk worthy of Him until all the struggles are over and we see Him face to face whom we love so dearly heart to heart!

Happy Flying!

Waken
  sleeping butterflies,
Burst your narrow prison.
Spread your golden wings and rise,
Spread your wings and tell the story,
How He rose,
  the Lord of glory.

M. R. Lathbury

Thanks to my "balcony people" . . .

My family—for always encouraging me to be myself and loving me in spite of it!

Joe and Barbara Ivey—who took me into their home and their hearts.

Cathy Cave and Martha Maughon—who listen.

Pat Berryhill—my prayer partner and one of the most beautiful examples of a flight attendant that I know.

Billy and Sandy Browning—who loved me onto a new plateau.

Ie Ie Longsdorf—who typed this manuscript with love.

Norma Baily—who kept me from getting too serious with myself as she proofread this book before it went to the editors.

Walter and Margy Sandell—who practice what they preach.

Jim Johnson—who was the first person to tell me that I should write a book and really believed I could.

Bill Gothard—who gave me a bigger view of God and His Word.

Bruce Larson and Keith Miller—whose writings gave me the courage to come out of my cocoon and write this book.

Carol Holquist—whose friendship and encouragement is much more than "just a job."

Judy Markham—my dear editor and friend who knows my heart.

And to all the people in the Fellowship of Christian Airline Personnel as well as other friends whose lives are more encouraging than I can ever tell.

"You Can Fly" and "I Give My Heart" are used by permission of Dj Butler.

"He Couldn't Be Safe" by Margaret Avison and "Restoration" by Renee Ashby are reprinted by permission of HIS, student magazine of Inter-Varsity Christian Fellowship.

The poem by M. R. Lathbury on page 135 is used by permission of Abbey Press.

The author appears in uniform on the back dust jacket with permission of Delta Air Lines, Inc.

A Special Tribute

Just a few days before this book went to press, my family and I passed an unusual milestone in our lives. As you have already read, my family means everything to me. Next to Jesus Christ in my life, their love and support have picked me up many times when my life was in pieces. They are truly the most important "balcony people" in my life.

A few days ago my two brothers were playing tennis. James, my twin, was about to serve the ball to John when he felt a pain in his upper chest. Thinking he had pulled a muscle, they stopped for a few minutes of rest. As the pain worsened, they headed for home. John and my sister-in-law Sandy took James to the hospital. Within two hours of that tennis game, my brother was dead. Medical cause of death: medial cystic necrosis. In layman's terms, his aorta had ruptured. And although this is a rare thing, it was even more unusual because it usually happens to persons in their seventies or eighties. My brother was forty years old and the picture of health. The doctors were as shocked as we.

Later, in explaining what happened, the doctor in attendance assured us there was nothing that could humanly have been done to save my brother's life. The doctor concluded: "He was destined for this."

The pain of loss is so acute that it would be unbearable if not for two factors. First, we know that our dear one is with Jesus Christ. That fact overrides any emotional void we feel. And second, there is no pain so deep, no loss so great that the love and peace of God does not go deeper still.

As I look at James's wife, Sandy, I see a peace and acceptance that is not of this world. Looking at my mother, I sense a love that is supernatural, one that overcomes grief. As I observe my brother John and especially my brother's children, I know that God is pouring out His grace and compassion in torrents. And the peace that I know cannot be described.

My one regret is that James never read this book, and I so wanted him to. Although he already knew some of the things I have written about, there were many facts about my life that he didn't know. But somehow I believe James already knows everything that is in this book. I imagine him in the balcony of heaven, urging me on, cheering me to stand firm in my convictions. He did that in his earthly life; I believe he is doing it now.

And the most glorious thing of all is that for James there is no more struggle—no more cocoon. He, now, knows what it *really* means to fly.

Thank you for the consistency of your life, James Roy Barfield. Thank you for *living* what you believed. Thank you for showing us in death, as in life, that our only hope is Him.

Janice Barfield
February 24, 1981

JANICE BARFIELD has been a flight attendant with Delta Air Lines for seventeen years, with her home base in Atlanta, Georgia. She was actively involved in the organization of The Fellowship of Christian Airline Personnel and was editor of their publication for several years. Janice enjoys free-lance writing and has published articles and poetry; several of her poems were included in the anthology of Christian verse, *God, I Like You.* *You Can Fly!* is her first book.

CHRISTIAN HERALD ASSOCIATION AND ITS MINISTRIES

CHRISTIAN HERALD ASSOCIATION, founded in 1878, publishes The Christian Herald Magazine, one of the leading interdenominational religious monthlies in America. Through its wide circulation, it brings inspiring articles and the latest news of religious developments to many families. From the magazine's pages came the initiative for CHRISTIAN HERALD CHILDREN'S HOME and THE BOWERY MISSION, two individually supported not-for-profit corporations.

CHRISTIAN HERALD CHILDREN'S HOME, established in 1894, is the name for a unique and dynamic ministry to disadvantaged children, offering hope and opportunities which would not otherwise be available for reasons of poverty and neglect. The goal is to develop each child's potential and to demonstrate Christian compassion and understanding to children in need.

Mont Lawn is a permanent camp located in Bushkill, Pennsylvania. It is the focal point of a ministry which provides a healthful "vacation with a purpose" to children who without it would be confined to the streets of the city. Up to 1000 children between the ages of 7 and 11 come to Mont Lawn each year.

Christian Herald Children's Home maintains year-round contact with children by means of an *In-City Youth Ministry.* Central to its philosophy is the belief that only through sustained relationships and demonstrated concern can individual lives be truly enriched. Special emphasis is on individual guidance, spiritual and family counseling and tutoring. This follow-up ministry to inner-city children culminates for many in financial assistance toward higher education and career counseling.

THE BOWERY MISSION, located at 227 Bowery, New York City, has since 1879 been reaching out to the lost men on the Bowery, offering them what could be their last chance to rebuild their lives. Every man is fed, clothed and ministered to. Countless numbers have entered the 90-day residential rehabilitation program at the Bowery Mission. A concentrated ministry of counseling, medical care, nutrition therapy, Bible study and Gospel services awakens a man to spiritual renewal within himself.

These ministries are supported solely by the voluntary contributions of individuals and by legacies and bequests. Contributions are tax deductible. Checks should be made out either to CHRISTIAN HERALD CHILDREN'S HOME or to THE BOWERY MISSION.

Administrative Office: 40 Overlook Drive, Chappaqua, New York 10514
Telephone: (914) 769-9000

You Can Fly!

What is life like at 30,000 feet?
Were the coffee-tea-or-me girls right?

The mystique of the glamorous mile-high world of the airline stewardess has intrigued and fascinated the earthbound since the day the Wright brothers left Kitty Hawk.

Flight attendant Janice Barfield is the ideal person to dispel the myths, for she has been flying with a major airline for seventeen years. During that time she has seen just about everything: from a passenger's dentures in a "discomfort" bag to emergencies such as illness and death. In YOU CAN FLY! she uses many of her experiences, both on the ground and in the air, to show what the life of a "stew" is really like.

But YOU CAN FLY! is much more than the personal experiences of a flight attendant. It is the story of a courageous young woman who truly wants to integrate her faith and her daily life. With freshness and candor, the author shares her real-life struggles with fear, failure, choosing a career, her own sexuality, servanthood, and singleness.

A unique inspirational book that will make you laugh and cry and learn a bit more about how to handle your own frustrations, disappointments, joys, and expectations.